CAREERS
IN ART

VGM Professional Careers Series

CAREERS
IN ART

BLYTHE CAMENSON

VGM Career Horizons
NTC/Contemporary Publishing Group

Library of Congress Cataloging-in-Publication Data

Camenson, Blythe.
    Careers in art / Blythe Camenson.
        p.   cm. — (VGM professional careers series)
      ISBN 0-658-00027-6 (cloth). — ISBN 0-658-00028-4 (paper)
      1. Art—Vocational guidance.   I. Title. II. Series.
  N8350.C34   1999
  702'.3'73—dc21   99-19985
                                                  CIP

Cover photograph copyright © PhotoDisc, Inc.

Published by VGM Career Horizons
A division of NTC/Contemporary Publishing Group, Inc.
4255 West Touhy Avenue, Lincolnwood (Chicago), Illinois 60712-1975 U.S.A.
Copyright © 2000 by NTC/Contemporary Publishing Group, Inc.
All rights reserved. No part of this book may be reproduced, stored in a
retrieval system, or transmitted in any form or by any means, electronic,
mechanical, photocopying, recording, or otherwise, without the prior written
permission of NTC/Contemporary Publishing Group, Inc.
Printed in the United States of America
International Standard Book Number: 0-658-00027-6 (cloth)
                                        0-658-00028-4 (paper)

00 01 02 03 04 HP 19 18 17 16 15 14 13 12 11 10 9 8 7 6 5 4 3 2 1

CONTENTS

ABOUT THE AUTHOR

A full-time writer of career books, Blythe Camenson's main professional concern is helping job seekers make educated choices. She firmly believes that with enough information, readers can find long-term, satisfying careers. To that end, she researches traditional as well as unusual occupations, talking to a variety of professionals about what their jobs are really like. In all her books she includes firsthand accounts from people who reveal what to expect in each occupation, the upsides as well as the down.

Camenson's interests range from history and photography to writing novels. She is also director of Fiction Writer's Connection, a membership organization providing support to new and published writers, and maintains a website at http://www.fictionwriters.com.

Camenson was educated in Boston, earning her B.A. in English and psychology from the University of Massachusetts and her M.Ed. in counseling from Northeastern University.

In addition to *Careers in Art*, Blythe Camenson has written more than three dozen books for NTC/Contemporary Publishing Group. She is also coauthor of *Your Novel Proposal: From Creation to Contract* (Writer's Digest Books).

ACKNOWLEDGMENTS

I would like to thank the following professionals for providing insights into the world of art careers:

Jim Anderson, stained-glass artist

Edwin Ryan Bailey, artist and art instructor

Matthew Carone, art gallery owner

Aileen Chuk, associate registrar

Mindy Conley, art teacher

Karen Duvall, graphic designer

Elizabeth English, artist and illustrator; art gallery curator

Joan Gardner, chief conservator

Erica Hirshler, assistant curator

Deb Mason, potter

Peggy Peters, art teacher

Lynne Robins, art teacher

Rodney Stephens, framemaker

CAREERS
IN ART

INTRODUCTION

Successful artists might tell you that they never consciously chose a career in art—the profession chose them. Although skill in creating art is something that can be learned, refined, and honed, many people feel they came to their work with an inborn talent; it was just something they could always do.

Whether art is something you never questioned would be your niche in life, an interest you discovered, or a skill you actively sought out, the career choices for you are numerous. In this book you will learn about the variety of settings in which you can work as an artist and the variety of job titles you can call yourself.

ART AS A COLLABORATIVE EFFORT

Human beings have been expressing themselves through art since the beginning of recorded history. The need to create and to share those creations has been an all-consuming force that even a millennium or two has not suppressed.

Early cave paintings suggest a collaborative effort. For each clan artist (except for the first) there must have been a teacher, a mentor, and a clan historian—the storyteller who passed on significant events from one generation to another. Perhaps there was even a color and design expert to discuss pigment and the most aesthetic placement of drawings upon the walls.

The image of the starving artist painting alone in a garret belies the fact that, today, collaboration continues. Artists study and are influenced by those who came before them. Other artists, also called art historians, delve deeply into the art of past and more recent cultures, then share that knowledge through their writings and teachings. Art educators also contribute, teaching budding artists of any age the time-tested techniques and methods for creating a variety of art—from ceramics to computer graphics.

Even art critics add to the collaborative effort, albeit inadvertently, helping to shape public tastes with their opinions. Museum curators and art gallery owners further the cause, choosing which art to display, which artist to promote.

Although many think of the creation of art as an individual effort, art does not stand alone. It functions in its own ecosystem, in which each component—like the water we drink and the air we breathe—is essential to the survival of the whole.

Where you can fit into this system is an individual choice, based on your interests and skills and desires, but the choices are varied. The degree of talent and skill you possess, the area that interests you, the amount of time you are willing to devote to study, the setting in which you prefer to work, and the kind of income you hope to earn will all influence the career path you choose.

But before you commit yourself to a path, explore it first. And if possible, begin that exploration at the beginning, with the question of education and training.

IS AN ART DEGREE NECESSARY?

For the gifted prodigy, probably not. This rare individual can work alone and produce magnificent works of art. But even those who are extremely talented can still benefit from professional training. Learning about other artists can help shape our own creations. Having the positive influence of a mentor can help introduce the art student to new techniques and media.

Not all artists create art for art's sake; studio art is not the only path to follow. Many careers in art require a degree: graphic artists, art educators, art curators, art historians, art restorers, art critics, and even art sellers must receive professional training and aquire experience to compete in the job market for these very popular fields.

In reality, most successful artists have pursued some form of higher education to hone their talent. Because educational options are as varied as the different careers in art, you must carefully consider which art program is right for you.

CHOOSING THE RIGHT ART PROGRAM

There are almost as many different names and focuses for art programs as there are job possibilities. Some common names are applied arts, fine arts, cyberarts, computer arts, computer-aided design, studio arts, art education, art history, museum studies, commercial arts, graphic arts, industrial arts, design, communication arts, and visual arts.

Art schools, institutes, colleges, and universities categorize their art programs in a variety of ways. In some institutions you will find the art department encased within colleges of liberal arts or humanities departments. Others have separate art schools. Still others combine art programs within the school of architecture, or with advertising, public relations, or other related disciplines.

The program or department name does not always obviously convey its focus. An aspiring art teacher would waste precious time enrolling in an art studies program that emphasized commercial art or design.

Many university programs allow for a great deal of latitude in designing majors and courses of study. It is now common practice to offer interdisciplinary degrees.

Art majors wishing to teach can take advantage of the interdisciplinary approach. It can be particularly helpful with the decisions future art educators must make concerning their studies. Should they pursue a B.F.A. in their chosen subject area, then work toward a teaching credential? Or should they study art education with a concentration in one of the subject areas?

There is no single correct answer. These decisions must be made individually, based on research into specific programs, personal long-term goals, and the availability of local programs or the ability to relocate if necessary.

As examples, several art programs at various institutions are highlighted here to show how different institutions focus their curricula. But, ultimately, you must continue this research, requesting catalogs, visiting campuses, and talking to other students and faculty members. An informed decision about your training program will only enhance your career opportunities.

SAMPLE ART PROGRAMS

Art Education K–12: University of Toledo, Ohio

You may, through the completion of 191 to 192 hours, become certified in Ohio to teach art in kindergarten through twelfth grade. The art education program of study is designed to develop your knowledge and skills as a student, teacher, and artist. A broad foundation in the liberal arts is an important facet of a strong education. With this in mind, you must complete 55 to 57 hours of general education. A critical element in the development of effective teachers is a strong professional background in the fundamentals of education. During this component of the program, which totals 26 hours, you not only will be introduced to the history, philosophy, and psychology of education, but also will have the opportunity to work in public schools to begin to get a feel for actual teaching. Course work of 10 hours in art education for the elementary classroom introduces you to methods and techniques for teaching art skills, art history, art criticism, and aesthetics. The 25-hour professional sequence in art education provides the final phase of teacher preparation. During these courses, you will be involved in numerous field-based instructional opportunities, including student teaching.

Central to the program of study is the development of your skills as an artist. Specific content areas of study include 25 hours of two-dimensional studies such as drawing, painting, computer graphics, design, and printmaking, 9 hours in three-dimensional studies such as ceramics, metals, and sculpture; and 18 hours in studio electives. Study of the history of art, which may include international travel, provides the final 15 hours of course studies.

Finally, your program of study will be completed by selecting an additional 18 hours of concentrated course work in studio art, art history, or art education.

The University of Toledo also has art programs in cyberarts, photography, sculpture, ceramics, painting, metals, printmaking, drawing, and art history.

Rhode Island School of Design

One of the most prestigious schools in the United States, the Rhode Island School of Design offers programs in the following areas: apparel, architecture, art education, ceramics, film and video, foundations of art, furniture, glass, graphic design, illustration, industrial arts, interactive arts, jewelry, landscape architecture, painting, photography, printmaking, sculpture, and textiles.

Rice University, Houston, Texas

Rice, founded in 1912 by William Marsh Rice, is a small private university dedicated to the promotion of letters and the arts, science, and engineering. Throughout its history, first as Rice Institute and later as Rice University, the institution has enjoyed a reputation for excellence and selectivity in a quiet and spacious campus setting. Current enrollment is about 2,700 undergraduates and 1,200 graduate students, numbers that maintain a remarkable one-to-ten faculty-student ratio.

Rice's president has observed, "We are extraordinarily fortunate in the setting provided for our pursuit of liberal as well as technical learning. On the campus as a whole, we are able to be a community of inquiry that allows, encourages, and even requires the collaboration among students and faculty that characterizes education at its best."

Within easy walking distance are the Museum of Fine Arts, the Contemporary Arts Museum, and the Museum of Natural Science.

Rice offers a unique environment—the personal atmosphere of a small liberal arts college and the intellectual stimulation of a research university within a large, lively, and diverse urban center.

Rice's School of Humanities houses the Art and Art History Department, which awards the following degrees: B.A. and B.F.A. in art history, studio art, film and photography, and archaeology; M.A. in teaching; and M.A. in art history and classical archaeology.

For students interested in teaching in secondary schools, a program of teacher training leading to certification in the State of Texas may be completed together with the B.A. degree. This program is administered by Rice's Department of Education.

Art History: University of Michigan, Ann Arbor

The history of art is a rich and multifaceted discipline, embracing the entire course of human history. Within this broad field are many areas of specialization, but overarching issues define a unified sense of purpose among all art historians. The concentration in the history of art at the University of Michigan is designed both to introduce students to a diverse repertoire of art from wide-ranging cultures and to expose students to a number of specialties in greater depth. In general terms, the goal of the undergraduate program is to enable every student to acquire the following skills and knowledge: a familiarity with some of the great works of painting, sculpture, and architecture produced by the civilizations of the world; an awareness of the religious or personal values and of the intellectual and social conditions that surrounded or are embodied in these works of art; an awareness of the ways the making of works of art—indeed, of all humanmade things—has grown or evolved in the course of time; a grasp of the nature of the concept of quality; the ability to analyze the qualities of works of art and also the qualities of the buildings, streets, and everyday objects that lie outside museum walls; the capacity to enter into the spirit of works of art that are culturally (and geographically or chronologically) distant and to draw conclusions about the aims and intentions of their makers; a sense of the rich history and varied methodological approaches of the discipline; and the ability to express feelings and impressions about art.

Minneapolis College of Art and Design

The design curriculum at MCAD teaches students how to identify and approach design problems, find creative and responsible solutions, and execute those solutions with precision and flair.

All design students start with courses that examine the general principles of design and techniques used by the designer. These courses draw from disciplines such as sociology, psychology, and anthropology to help students better understand cultural influences and their future clients.

In studio classes, students apply this knowledge and develop technical skills in hands-on projects. Through creative exercises they learn the techniques required for professional practice.

In the areas of graphic design, illustration, and advertising design students generate ideas and imagery, use color, integrate images and text, and explore the dynamics of typography and page composition.

Furniture design students approach their studies from three key points of view: the creation of individual pieces from the artist's expression, the mastering of the ability to design for a specific purpose or patronage, and the skills of relating individualized designs to industrial processes.

Students with a graphic design, furniture design, or advertising specialization are required to take computer graphics courses. Computers are used in most design classes to produce work and are important tools for exploring and experimenting with alternative methods of solving typography and image problems. All design majors are required to take theory and methodology courses and to complete a senior project.

Visual Arts: The School of Art, Montana State University, Bozeman

Montana State University houses the School of Art, a professional school within the College of Art and Architecture. The department offers courses leading to a B.A. degree with programs in ceramics, jewelry and metalsmithing, painting, drawing, graphic design, sculpture, art history, and art education. Montana State also offers an M.F.A. degree in ceramics, jewelry and metalsmithing, painting, drawing, and sculpture. The professional art program at Montana State enjoys a national reputation and offers the training and personal guidance necessary for a successful career in the visual arts. All programs are accredited by the National Association of Schools of Art and Design.

YOUR CAREER OPTIONS

The aim of this book is to help you narrow the wide range of choices and find the career path that best suits your education, interests, and skills.

This book explores five main art career options. Although it is not exhaustive, this list of main tracks comprises hundreds of different job titles. Many are explored throughout the following chapters under these primary categories:

Graphic Arts

Fine Arts

Art Education

Museum Studies

Art Sales

As mentioned earlier, this list is by no means exhaustive. As you read, research, and talk to other working artists and art educators, you may unearth several other possibilities for yourself.

Also, as you read many of the firsthand accounts included in the chapters ahead, you will see that often artists don't limit themselves to one particular career track. Portrait artists also design T-shirts. Potters work in living history museums. Graphic artists do stints in art galleries. Sculptors work in advertising agencies.

Whichever track you ultimately choose, your decision to be flexible will ultimately broaden your employment options.

SAMPLE JOB LISTINGS

As a preview, take a look at the following samples of actual job listings. They offer an overview of the types of duties you would perform and the working conditions you can expect. They also specify the training you would need to qualify.

Position: Art Director

A leader in the casual entertainment software industry is seeking a senior art director to join our team. Individual will be responsible for the art direction and design of classic games software titles. This hands-on creative position involves overseeing creative development, defining the look and feel of the product, and supervising artists. Primary production responsibilities include 2D design and illustration; knowledge of 3D helpful. Requires technical knowledge of art tools (Photoshop, DeBabelizer, FreeHand, After Effects) and development engines. Industrial design, graphic design, or related degree required. Minimum four to five years of professional design and supervisory experience. Familiarity with Internet applications a plus.

Position: Web Production Artist

A high-profile Internet commerce leader needs full-time Web production artist to create banners, scan and touch up artwork, create original elements for the existing site, and contribute to the design of our new site slated for next year. Immediate opening. We're looking for someone who is creative and highly organized, has a great sense of humor, and understands the power of good design. We need someone who already has strong Photoshop, ImageReady, DeBabelizer, and scanning skills as well as a good understanding of image compression and Web palette issues. (Flash and HTML skills are a plus.) Must be Windows and Mac literate. Benefits include a stock plan as well as medical, dental, and vision insurance.

Position: Senior Designer for Travel Magazine

A national consumer magazine has a position for a full-time graphic designer. Applicants must have magazine experience and interest in travel. This is a full-time salaried position. The salary range is $30,000–36,000 depending on experience.

Position: Graphic Designer

Hip interactive point-of-purchase merchandising company seeks flexible graphic designer to help bring hot new projects to life. Candidates must be familiar with the latest graphic design and DTP tools (Photoshop, Illustrator, PageMaker, Quark XPress, etc.), but, ideally, also be able to do some work with traditional materials. If you're ready to exercise creative license and can thrive in a dynamic environment, send your resume to us.

Position: Graphic Artist

With over 600 retail superstores and record-breaking sales of more than $6.7 billion, our growth continues. Join us now in our fast-paced advertising department. Requires proficiency in Quark XPress with a minimum of five years' experience. Knowledge of retail advertising for production of catalogs, direct mail, and newspapers a plus. We offer competitive compensation and excellent benefits including 401(k) plan, on-site cafeteria, and a business casual working environment.

Position: Illustrator

A well-established greeting card company seeks talented illustrator and cartoonist. Prior related experience preferred. B.F.A. or M.F.A. preferred but successful portfolio may substitute for formal degree. Starting salary in the mid-$30s. Send cover letter, resume, and slides.

Position: Art Curator

Opening for a curator of visual resources; reports to assistant director, collection development and curatorial projects. Develops coherent plan for managing collection of 1.75 million study photographs of art and architecture. Implements organizational, cataloging, and preservation work plans to enhance scholarly understanding and accessibility. Participates in museum's overall collection development programs, acts as subject bibliographer, and recommends acquisitions of special collections and visual resources materials. Conducts scholarly research, provides advanced reference, and participates in activities including exhibitions, lectures, and publications. Requires Ph.D. in art history or related humanities discipline, or equivalent combination of training and experience; comprehensive knowledge of the history of art with two or more specialized research fields within the broad areas of Mediterranean archaeology and European art from the Middle Ages to the nineteenth century; fluency in relevant languages plus reading ability in two other western European languages.

Position: Exhibits Registrar

Registrar is responsible for creating, organizing, and maintaining orderly forms, legal documents, files, and retrieval systems. Organizes, documents, and coordinates all aspects of borrowing and lending objects, including handling, packing, and shipping of objects. Will supervise implementation of a collections management database and maintain the database and records associated with the art collection. Required qualifications: bachelor's degree or equivalent; minimum two years' experience in museum registration, fine arts shipping, or related experience; knowledge of conservation and storage practices, legal matters related to the collection, copyright laws and policies governing rights and reproductions, insurance requirements for the collections, and packing techniques and transportation methods; demonstrated ability to plan and implement multiple projects and work independently; flexibility in originating sound solutions; ability to work in an organized manner; ability to travel two to three weeks at a time.

Position: Exhibits Technician

One of the nation's most prominent and historic sites has an excellent opportunity for a hands-on individual with experience in building and maintaining exhibits and handling artifacts. Requires minimum two years' relevant experience and proficiency in carpentry, fabrication, and basic art skills. An interest in U.S. military history is a plus. We offer competitive salary and benefits.

Position: Art Instructor

Full-time art instructor to instruct freshman and sophomore art theory and studio courses within a one-person department. Minimum requirements are a master's degree in education with twenty-four hours' concentration in art or an M.F.A. Preference for community college experience. Eligible for state postsecondary licensure. Salary commensurate with experience.

Position: Art Educator

Fixed-term, one-year position. Ph.D. in art education preferred. Teach undergraduate art education and participate in the elementary program. Advising, relevant research, creative work, and service to community expected. The Art Department employs ten faculty members and offers over 240 majors for B.A., B.S., B.F.A., M.A., and M.S. degrees. NASAD accredited. Excellent resources, library, gallery, visiting artist program.

Position: Art Instructor, Sculpture/Ceramics

College seeks applications for a two-year non-tenure-track term position at the assistant professor level beginning September. Teaching responsibilities will include two offerings each of beginning to intermediate sculpture, beginning to intermediate ceramics, and a 2D/3D design course. M.F.A. in sculpture (preferred) or ceramics and a minimum of two years of college-level teaching experience required. Salary competitive and consistent with level of experience. Candidates are expected to have high aptitude and interest in undergraduate teaching, a commitment to the liberal arts, and a desire to involve undergraduates in creative work both inside and outside the classroom. Send letter of application, curriculum vitae, slide portfolio of recent work, undergraduate and graduate transcripts (unofficial acceptable), a detailed statement of teaching philosophy and goals, and three letters of recommendation.

YOUR JOB SEARCH

The sample job listings give you an idea of what's out there. When you are ready to start your job search, you can use conventional methods like newspaper ads, word of mouth, the Internet, job and recruitment fairs, direct calls, and blind resume submissions. But each job discussed in this book also has its own avenues to pursue. The following chapters will lead you to those avenues and get you started in the right direction.

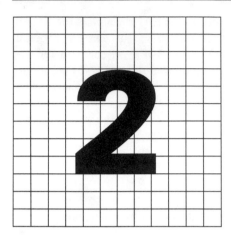

GRAPHIC ARTS

The term "visual arts" covers the fields of graphic arts and illustration as well as studio or fine arts. This chapter focuses on careers in graphic arts; the next chapter discusses studio or fine arts.

Graphic artists (also known as commercial artists) and illustrators offer their artistic skills and vision to commercial clients such as major corporations, retail stores, and advertising, design, or publishing firms. Their lot in life is much more secure than that of the studio or fine artist, although a regular paycheck often means sacrificing some of the artistic freedom the studio artists enjoy.

Graphic artists, whether freelancers or employed by a firm, use a variety of print, electronic, and film media to create art that meets a client's needs. Graphic artists are increasingly using computers instead of the traditional tools such as pens, pencils, scissors, and color strips to produce their work. Computers enable them to lay out and test various designs, formats, and colors before printing a final design.

WHAT GRAPHIC ARTISTS DO

Graphic artists perform different jobs depending on their areas of expertise and the needs of their employers. Some work for only one employer; other graphic artists freelance and work for a variety of clients.

Graphic designers, who usually design on a two-dimensional level, may create packaging and promotional displays for a new product, the visual design for an annual report and other corporate literature, or a distinctive logo for a product or business. They also help with the layout and design of magazines, newspapers, journals, and other publications, and create graphics for television.

Illustrators paint or draw pictures for books, magazines, and other publications; films; and paper products, including greeting cards, calendars, wrapping paper, and stationery. Many create a variety of illustrations, while others specialize in a particular style.

Medical and scientific illustrators combine artistic skills with knowledge of the biological sciences. Medical illustrators draw human anatomy and surgical procedures. Scientific illustrators draw animals and plants. These illustrations are used in medical and scientific publications, and in audiovisual presentations for teaching purposes. Medical illustrators also work for lawyers, producing exhibits for court cases, and for physicians.

Fashion artists draw women's, men's, and children's clothing and accessories for newspapers, magazines, and other media.

Storyboard illustrators draw storyboards for TV commercials. Storyboards present TV commercials in a series of scenes similar to a comic strip, so an advertising agency and client (the company doing the advertising) can evaluate proposed commercials. Storyboards may also serve as guides to the placement of actors and cameras and to other details during the production of commercials.

Cartoonists draw political, advertising, social, and sports cartoons. Some cartoonists collaborate with writers. Most cartoonists, however, have humorous, critical, or dramatic talents in addition to their drawing skills.

Animators work in the motion picture and television industries. They draw by hand and use computers to create the large series of pictures that, when transferred to film or tape, form the animated cartoons seen in movies and on TV.

Art directors, also called **visual journalists**, review the text of periodicals, newspapers, and other printed media and decide how to visually present the information in an eye-catching yet organized manner. They make decisions about which photographs or artwork to use and generally oversee production of the printed material.

WORKING LIFESTYLES

Graphic artists work in art and design studios located in office buildings or in their own homes. Graphic artists employed by publishing companies and art and design studios generally work a standard forty-hour week. During busy periods, they may work overtime to meet deadlines.

Self-employed graphic artists can set their own hours but may spend much time and effort selling their services to potential customers or clients and establishing a reputation. Many graphic artists work part-time as freelancers while continuing in a full-time job until they become established. Others have enough talent, perseverance, and confidence in their abilities to start freelancing full-time immediately after they graduate from art school. Many take on freelance projects while still enrolled in school in order to gain experience and acquire a portfolio of published work.

The successful freelance artist develops a set of clients who regularly contract for work. Some freelancers are widely recognized for their skill in specialties such as children's book illustration, magazine illustration, or design. These artists can earn high incomes and can pick and choose the type of work they do.

But most freelance careers take time to build. While making contacts and developing skills, many find work in various organizations. Still other commercial artists prefer full-time employment over freelancing.

EMPLOYMENT SETTINGS

Full-time graphic artists can find work in a variety of settings.

Advertising Agencies and Design Firms

People hired by advertising agencies or graphic design studios often start with relatively routine work. During this time, however, they may observe and practice their skills on the side. Jobs can cover anything from direct-mail pieces to catalog work, posters, and even aspects of the television and motion picture industries.

Publishing Companies

Magazine, newspaper, and book publishers require the expertise of commercial artists for a wide range of duties. These include cover design, advertising layout, typesetting, and graphics.

Department Stores

Department stores, especially the larger chains, routinely produce catalogs, direct-mail pieces, fliers, posters, and a variety of other advertising and promotional material. While small stores might send the work out to freelancers, large department stores often have fully staffed departments to handle the workload.

The Television and Motion Picture Industries

This is wide-open territory. Organizations such as Disney, for example, actively recruit new graduates right out of art schools and offer very attractive salaries. Opportunities are especially strong for those versed in computer graphics.

Other Businesses and Government Agencies

Other settings include manufacturing firms and the various agencies within the local, state, and federal government.

THE QUALIFICATIONS YOU'LL NEED

Graphic Arts

In the graphic arts field, demonstrated ability and appropriate training or other qualifications are needed for success. Evidence of talent and skill shown in the portfolio is an important factor used by art and design directors and others in deciding whether to hire or offer a contract to an artist. The portfolio is a collection of handmade, computer-generated, or printed examples of the artist's best work. In theory, a person with a good portfolio but no training or experience could succeed in graphic arts. In reality, assembling an impressive portfolio requires skills generally developed in a postsecondary art or design school program, such as a bachelor's degree program in fine arts, graphic design, or visual communications.

Internships also provide excellent opportunities for artists and designers to develop and enhance their portfolios. Most programs in art and design also provide training in computer design techniques. This training is becoming increasingly important as a qualification for many jobs in commercial art.

Medical Illustration

The appropriate training and education for prospective medical illustrators is more specific. Medical illustrators must not only demonstrate artistic ability but also have a detailed knowledge of living organisms, surgical and medical procedures, and human and sometimes animal anatomy. A four-year bachelor's degree combining art and premedical courses is usually required, followed by a master's degree in medical illustration, a degree offered in only a few accredited schools in the United States.

THE JOB HUNT

As in most any professional career, contacts and having a foot in the door at the type of organization for which you'd like to work are valuable assets. Internships are pathways to both.

The best strategy is to plan ahead. During your undergraduate or graduate studies, arrange for as many internships as you can squeeze in—either full-time during the summers or part-time during semesters.

An internship at an advertising agency, PR firm, or TV studio will give you a broad overview of that field; it will also help you build a successful portfolio. If an internship gives you a foot in the door, a professional and creative portfolio can open that door all the way. In addition, find yourself a mentor, someone who can critique your portfolio and advise you on how best to proceed.

GETTING AHEAD

In general, illustrators advance as their work circulates and as they establish a reputation for a particular style. The best illustrators continue to try new ideas, and their work constantly evolves over time.

Graphic artists within firms may advance to assistant art director, art director, design director, and in some companies, creative director of an art or design department. Some may gain enough skill to succeed as freelancers or they may prefer to specialize in a particular area. Others decide to open their own businesses.

INCOME

The Society of Publication Designers estimates that typical entry-level graphic designers earned between $23,000 and $27,000 annually in 1997. Earnings for self-employed graphic artists vary widely. Those struggling to gain experience and a reputation may be forced to charge close to the minimum wage for their work. Well-established freelancers may earn much more than salaried artists. Like other independent workers, however, self-employed artists must provide their own health insurance benefits.

CAREER OUTLOOK

Employment of graphic artists is expected to grow faster than the average for all occupations through the year 2006. Visual artists held about 276,000 jobs in 1996.

Nearly six out of ten were self-employed. Most self-employed graphic artists free-lanced, offering their services to advertising agencies, publishing firms, and other businesses.

Of the graphic artists who were not self-employed, many worked for advertising agencies, design firms, commercial art and reproduction firms, or printing and publishing firms. Other artists were employed by the motion picture and television industries, wholesale and retail trade establishments, and public relations firms.

INTERVIEW

Elizabeth English
Artist/Illustrator

Elizabeth English provides some valuable insights about getting started and what the work really involves. As you'll see, she is like many artists who have worked in a variety of settings. You can read her firsthand account of curating for an art gallery in Chapter 6. Here she talks about her freelance artist career.

How did you get started in this field?

I didn't choose the field of art, it chose me! I've been doing artwork since I could hold a crayon. I continued in the field in college because I enjoyed it and it was a satisfying way to express myself. And I had received a full scholarship to continue my studies in art. I never thought of doing anything else, along with the writing I also do.

I received my training in the field of art by majoring in art in high school, by attending college art courses as my major, by traveling around the world and looking at others' artwork, by being a curator in an art gallery, and by reading books on art.

But mostly, I just practiced my art, from drawing to painting and pottery, from sculpture to cartooning, from stained glass to weaving and also going on expeditions to archaeological sites and documenting prehistoric rock art and ethnic arts and crafts around the world.

Another way I was trained was by working as an artist in an advertising agency, creating logos, label designs, and ads. I also worked for a newspaper, where I did artwork for ads, designing characters and print campaigns. I was a cartoonist for the paper as well. I had many humorous and political/topical cartoons published.

I got my first job in the art field by having an art show during my senior year in high school, and all the works were sold. One of the buyers was the owner of an advertising agency, and he offered me a job as the agency artist (at a whopping one dollar per hour in 1960).

I am now working as a freelance artist. I am mostly involved in animation for feature films. Although I don't do the animation itself, I design the characters, backgrounds, costumes, interiors, and logos for the animated features. I also write the screenplays for them and write the lyrics for the songs.

I am also working as a fine artist and have had hundreds of my artworks placed in private homes. I work on commission for private clients. I do large-scale sculptures in metal, and paintings, tapestries, stained glass, pottery, and weavings. Occasionally, I design the art and have other artists create it under my supervision.

Another facet of my working in the arts is being an art consultant for individuals and corporations. I am paid to travel the world of museums and art galleries and artists' studios to purchase paintings, have them matted and framed properly, and install them in private homes, hotels, restaurants, offices, and even palaces in Saudi Arabia.

I am in the process of working up some illustrations for several children's books I have written, and will send them to publishers in the near future. I have also written a series of contemporary cartoons specifically for the *New Yorker* magazine. And I have several *New Yorker* magazine covers about ready to go.

I'm also writing and illustrating an encyclopedia of the art, lore, and mythology of mermaids, so there is a lot of travel and research, plus artwork, to be done for that.

I've written three feature film animation screenplays and am working on designing the characters and backgrounds for them. I am producing several documentary films, and, as the art director and production designer for those films, I have another opportunity to be creative and use my skills as an artist. I'm planning on doing some music videos in the near future, and that's even more creative—and lucrative.

For fifteen years, I used my skills and sensibilities as an artist in another profession: interior design. Color, balance, decoration, architecture all come into play when doing interior design.

Other ways I've used my knowledge and talent as an artist include working in theater as a set designer, costume designer, and lighting designer.

What's a typical day like?

I choose to do whatever project most interests me on any particular day—or, if I have a deadline, I focus on that project first.

I spend a lot of time finding clients, sending out query letters and examples of my work and credits, and later following up on those queries.

I also spend a lot of time designing artwork and making up sketches for client approvals. Often I design furniture for clients or hand-hooked rugs and tapestries.

What do you like most about working in this field?

My job is fascinating, satisfying, and creative, and I feel it helps others to see the world in a different way and to appreciate both the beauties of nature and their fellow human beings in a new light.

The day goes by so quickly when I am being an artist and either drawing, designing, painting, or whatever, that sometimes I work into the night without realizing that I forgot dinner.

I can work in the middle of the night, work eighteen hours without stopping, take days off if I feel like it. I can work wearing my robe and nightgown all day, or I can go for a hike with my dog and take my drawing or painting supplies and create art out in nature, observing the world.

Occasionally, I travel to Provence or Tuscany or Greece or Japan and paint or sketch there for a few weeks. I enjoy documenting prehistoric rock art at archaeological sites in the Southwest United States and in Patagonia. An artist is needed there, because a scientist cannot truly "see" the works as the original artist did.

I love having the opportunity to be creative and to express myself. Being an artist allows me to do that and make a living at the same time.

Another good thing about working as an artist is that most clients know very little about the arts, and you are left to do your work without interference or suggestions from the boss! I also like working freelance, because I can set my own hours and working situation. The pay is usually very good, and I have made a fine living as an artist for many years. Plus, I have the pleasure of seeing my work in people's homes and in offices, hotels, and other settings.

What are the downsides of working in this field?

In illustration, many clients want something specific and you must work to satisfy their needs rather than being wholly creative. Also, there is not as much money in illustration as in fine arts. In fine arts, however, it is very difficult to get your work sold, unless you have steady clientele or a big name.

How much money can someone in your field expect to earn?

I have not worked for a salary for so many years. Freelance is my preference. I have been paid $25,000 for one sculpture, $10,000 for a painting, $10,000 for stained glass, $5,000 for a weaving.

In illustration and cartooning, the pay is much lower, sometimes as little as $5 for a published cartoon or illustration, though that's for local work in hometown newspapers. A cover for the *New Yorker* pays many thousands, and the cartoons bring in around $500 to $1,000 each. Music videos pay up to $50,000 for artwork sometimes. A children's book illustration can earn anywhere from $1,000 to $10,000 or more, if it wins an award and is a bestseller.

What advice would you give to other artists?

Be creative always. Think like an artist. Live as an artist. Persevere and never give up. Read everything you can on the arts: books and magazines. Attend a good art school. Practice your art. Diversify! Be a painter, a sculptor. Do drawings using everything from crayons to charcoal to pencil to pen to Japanese brushwork.

Study the arts and methods of artists of other cultures and other times. Learn stained glass, pottery, and other crafts.

Go to museums, art shows, and gallery openings. Make up a great—not just good but *great*—portfolio of your best diversified artwork.

And read the book *The Artist's Way* by Julia Cameron and follow her advice.

Elizabeth English works as an artist/illustrator for a literary and film production company in Boulder, Colorado. She has been in the field for more than twenty years. She earned her B.F.A. at C. W. Post College in Greenvale, Long Island, New York, in 1976. She has also done substantial graduate work at a variety of institutions, including Hunter College; the State University of New York, Farmingdale; the University of Colorado in Boulder; and the Pratt Institute in Brooklyn.

INTERVIEW

Karen Duvall
Graphic Designer

How did you get started?

I started drawing at a very early age, since before I could even walk (according to my mother). I've known all my life that I would be an artist.

I enrolled at a school that focuses exclusively on graphic design. It was an intense two-year program with six-hour days of instruction each week, no summers off.

I was newly married and pregnant with my first child when I graduated from art school. I didn't get my first job until my daughter was six months old. One of my neighbors was an art teacher at a nearby elementary school and she hired me as her teacher's aide.

I've only been at my current job for about six months. I used to be the graphics manager for a gift manufacturer, until they decided it was too expensive to create packaging for their products. My layoff was sudden and unexpected, with no severance pay offered, so needless to say I was devastated. I'd never been laid off before, and I was suddenly without a job. I couldn't afford to be out of work, so I immediately began contacting everyone I knew in the business: other designers, dozens of printers I'd worked with over the course of my career, several service bureaus, a few ad agencies, and just about anyone else I could think of. I made good use of the Internet, placing my resume on-line and answering job ads posted on various career websites.

After about a week's worth of panic, I E-mailed a designer who once worked for me several years ago at a financial marketing firm. He's now the creative director for Publication Design, and it just so happened he was going out of town for a week and asked if I'd fill in for him while he was gone. I eagerly accepted the opportunity. After five days—on what was supposed to be my last day there—one of the other artists turned in his resignation. I was offered a full-time position, with an even higher salary than my previous job.

The moral of this story is to always keep track of the contacts you make in your field; you never know when you might need them.

What is your job like?

I'm lucky to have a position that's extremely creative, and because of my experience, my employer gives me free rein on the projects I undertake. The best way to describe my job is to give an example of a project I completed recently. One of our top clients asked me to come up with a promotional piece they could mail to prospects, something unique and very special. They had a big budget, so I was free to experiment with my ideas. I came up with a pop-up card, a very complicated design that was colorful, contained a direct message that got right to the point, and was three-dimensional when opened—giving it "staying power" (meaning it wouldn't be tossed in the trash the minute it was opened, like most direct-mail pieces).

While managing this project, I was involved in many client meetings, created several proofs for the client's approval, dealt directly with the printer who would manufacture the pop-up, checked prepress proofs, and did both a press check and a die-cut check on location. The client was ecstatic over the finished product, and the printer has entered it in the 1999 National Packaging Awards.

Our office atmosphere is casual; jeans and a T-shirt are typical attire, though we dress up a little for client meetings. It's a small company with a limited sales staff, one customer service rep, technicians for our prepress equipment and Sci-tex scanner, and six artists, two of whom are devoted exclusively to one weekly magazine.

Most of my projects are interesting, but not all are as involved as the one I just described. I often create brochures and ads for newspapers and magazines. We also design logos and corporate communication material, book covers, consumer product labels, training materials, etc. You name it, we'll design it.

All design and illustration is done on Macintosh computers, using such programs as Photoshop, Illustrator, Quark XPress, and Painter. All artists have Wacom tablets with a laser stylus for easy drawing and painting via the computer. The digital art files we create can become quite large, so our hard drives allow for several gigabytes of storage, and we have an immense archive system and several network servers.

For the most part, the atmosphere is relaxed, though it can become tense when deadlines approach or when there are equipment failures. We work a standard forty-hour week, but we may work overtime on occasion. All the artists have computers at home, so our employer allows us to take work home now and then and pays us overtime for the extra effort. We're lucky; most employers in this field won't allow overtime work to be done this way.

What's the best part of the job?

What I like most about my job is the creative freedom I have. I've been a designer long enough that I'm completely trusted in my design directions and the methods I use to develop my projects.

What's the worst part of the job?

What I like least are the clients who can't make up their minds and constantly make changes, so it's like doing a project completely over, again and again and again. I consider it a waste of valuable time. But at least we bill by the hour.

What is the typical salary for a graphic designer?

My salary falls between $35,000 and $40,000 per year. I'm paid by the hour, and overtime is calculated at time and half, so by the end of this year I may well exceed these numbers.

Graphic design salaries are typically unstructured; the pay scale is completely up to the employer. It also depends on the cost of living in your resident state. But take note that the industry is highly competitive. There's no lack of graphic artists for hire, but there is a demand for good ones. A good graphic artist is someone who can do more than draw pretty pictures. They must also be knowledgeable in client and vendor relations, have technical experience in the tools of the trade, be well-versed in all areas of prepress production, have an ability to conceptualize a solution to a visual communications problem, and have an optimistic attitude.

Here in Colorado, an artist just starting out can expect to earn anywhere from $8 to $12 an hour. Freelancers make far more than that, anywhere from $50 to $100 an hour, but freelance jobs are unpredictable and may not be able to supply you with a living wage. However, freelancing is a good way to supplement your regular income. Though I limit the number of freelance jobs I undertake (I can afford to be picky), it allows me great versatility and some pretty snappy samples for my portfolio.

How would you advise those considering a career in this field?

A successful graphic artist is one who pays his or her dues while moving up in the ranks. The graphic arts field is extremely broad and far more versatile than most people think. From personal experience, I've learned that changing jobs, broadening your range of skills, and dipping your toes into the various waters of the industry will create the most opportunities for your developing career.

Creative talent is your foundation for success, but you'll need far more than that to be truly successful. A good art school is an adequate start, but that education won't take you very far. Most schools are inept at providing you with the skills and expertise essential to making it in a real graphics job. They focus on the fun stuff, the creative puffery that does more for the ego than anything else, and end up inflating a fledgling artist's expectations of a successful graphics career. I personally have trained many recent graduates, most of whom had no clue how to function as a productive artist in the working world. So a school can only give you the bare basics; the rest is up to you.

If you're serious about pursuing a career in the graphic arts, I suggest you practice being a highly astute observer. Even while you're attending art school, you should still concentrate on your own self-education by meeting professionals in your chosen field and asking lots of questions. Request a tour of a print shop and have someone take you from prepress to stripping to platemaking, and then to the actual presses themselves. Ask questions such as: What are the biggest problems you encounter when working with graphic designers? What do you suggest that can help prevent me from making the same mistakes? Also, visit service bureaus and observe what actually goes into running electronic files to film. See how match prints are made, learn what an Iris is, and understand exactly how the four-color process works to create a full-color image. Do you know what a color build is? What's spot color? What's the difference between a sheetfed press and a web press, and how does the quality differ? What's digital printing, and is it better than offset? What line screen is best for printing your particular project? How is silk-screen printing done, and why are the process and inks used different from other methods of printing? What's flexography? What's thermography? What's the difference between aqueous coating and UV? This is all very basic stuff, all elements that can have a dramatic effect on your design, and very little of it will ever be covered in art school.

Graphic design goes far beyond the first step of creating something that looks nice. You must know and understand the end results of a printed piece of artwork before you can effectively initiate the creation of one.

Karen Duvall is a graphic designer with Publication Design Inc. in Denver, Colorado, a full-service design agency specializing in magazine publications. She has been in the field since 1978. She has an associate's degree in advertising design from the Colorado Institute of Art in Denver.

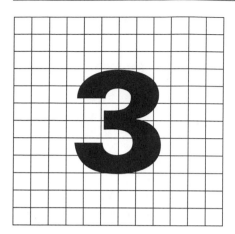

FINE ARTS

Your artistic talent has been practiced and honed through your art degree program and through your own hard work. Your goal has always been to support yourself as an artist or craftsperson—perhaps even to open your own studio, a place in which to create and sell your work. Whether it's pottery or painting, sewing or stained glass, you can make a name for yourself and work full-time in your chosen area—without necessarily starving in an artist's garret.

Having said that, few studio artists can move immediately into a career that provides adequate financial support, at least initially. It takes time to build a reputation or a clientele; during those "lean years," many artists seek out additional avenues where they can be assured of a regular paycheck.

Although some artists might moonlight in a number of different occupations—anything from food service to secretarial work—the vast majority choose to stay in related fields. Those with a teaching certificate may teach art in elementary or secondary schools, while those with a master's or doctoral degree may teach in colleges or universities.

Some fine artists work in arts administration in city, state, or federal arts programs. Others may work as art critics, as art consultants, or as directors or representatives in fine art galleries; as private art instructors; or as curators setting up art exhibits in museums. You will find talented artists working in a variety of settings, many of which are covered in this and other chapters in this book.

GOALS

For the serious studio artist, the main goal is to create a work of art that combines self-expression with the need to make a living. It can be done.

Fine arts (also known as studio arts) and graphic arts make up the two categories that fall under the umbrella of the visual arts. Their difference depends not so much on the medium as on the artist's purpose in creating a work of art. Graphic artists, many of whom own their own studios, put their artistic skills and vision at the service of commercial clients, such as major corporations, retail stores, and advertising, design, or publishing firms. Studio artists, on the other hand, often create art to satisfy their own need for self-expression; they may display their work in museums, corporate collections, art galleries, and private homes. Some of their work may be done on request from clients, but not as exclusively as graphic artists.

Fine artists usually work independently, choosing whatever subject matter and medium suits them. Usually, they specialize in one or two (or more) forms of art.

THE DISCIPLINES

Studio artists use an almost limitless variety of methods and materials to communicate ideas, thoughts, and feelings. They use oils, watercolors, acrylics, pastels, magic markers, pencils, pen and ink, silk screen, plaster, clay, or any of a number of other media, including computers, to create realistic and abstract works or images of objects, people, nature, topography, or events. The following examples describe just a few of the many fine arts disciplines.

Painters

These artists generally work with two-dimensional art forms. Using techniques of shading, perspective, and color-mixing, painters produce works that depict realistic scenes or may evoke different moods and emotions, depending on the artist's goals.

Sculptors

These three-dimensional artists either mold and join materials such as clay, glass, wire, plastic, or metal, or cut and carve forms from a block of plaster, wood, or stone. Some sculptors combine various materials such as concrete, metal, wood, plastic, and paper.

Potters

Working with a variety of clay materials—from low-fire clays to high-fire stoneware or porcelain—potters either handcraft their artwork or create different forms using a potter's wheel. They follow existing glaze recipes or experiment with different chemicals to formulate their own finishes.

Printmakers

Printmakers create printed images from designs cut into wood, stone, or metal, or from computer-driven data. The designs may be engraved as in the case of woodblocking; etched as in the production of etchings; or derived from computers in the form of ink-jet or laser prints.

Stained-Glass Artists

Working with glass, paints, leading, wood, and other materials, these artists create functional as well as decorative artwork such as windows, skylights, or doors.

Photographers   Photographers utilize their cameras, lenses, film, and darkroom chemicals the way painters use paint and canvas. They capture realistic scenes of people, places, and events, or through the use of various techniques, both natural and contrived, they create photographs that elicit a variety of moods and emotions.

GETTING AHEAD

Fine artists advance as their work circulates and as they establish a reputation for a particular style. The best artists continue to experiment with new ideas, and their work constantly evolves over time.

WORKING LIFESTYLES

Artists generally work in art and design studios located in commercial buildings or in their own home studios. Some artists prefer to work alone; others like working with other artists. For the latter group, sharing space with other artists is often a viable alternative to the lone studio—both for stimulation and for economics. The trend in many large cities and even in less populated areas is toward shared space in cooperatively owned studios or rented space in converted warehouses or storefronts.

While artists generally require well-lighted and ventilated surroundings, some art forms in particular demand an environment conducive to the odors and dust from glues, paint, ink, clay, or other materials.

INTERVIEW

Edwin Ryan Bailey
Studio Artist

How did you get started in this field?

Like most toddlers, I was fascinated with drawing. By second grade I was already answering the "What do you want to be when you grow up?" question with the occupation of artist. My parents and teachers recognized that I had a gift and fortunately encouraged it. There weren't any professional artists in the area where I grew up in rural Alabama, except for a few local women who taught private lessons.

In my junior year in high school in 1979 I opened my first art studio (Ryan's Art Studio, Lineville, Alabama). I took out a loan on my own and rented a building in my hometown. There I sold basic painting supplies and taught private art lessons. I had forty-five students, ages five to seventy-five. I also did commissioned paintings and portraits, and painted nearly all the new signs in town.

While I had the studio I taught myself to airbrush and started painting shirts. This opened up the possibility of making money at craft fairs—which I did on the weekends and in the summers. I really had no idea what an artist did or what types of jobs were out there. I simply created my own niche. I sold the business when I moved away for college.

As a child I had taken private lessons, but the real eye-opener came when I entered college at Auburn University. Many of my classmates had studied commercial art in high school, whereas I didn't even know what a T-square was. There were two options, fine arts or illustration/design. I took as many classes as I could in both fields.

Like most things worth doing, it is a continual process of upgrading oneself. I constantly study and try to learn new techniques and improve upon old ones. It requires continual practice.

To pay my way through college, I started airbrushing T-shirts again. I moved to the beach in the summer and worked at a T-shirt shop. I found I could do as well there as some of the graduates in my field could working year-round at the entry-level illustration jobs. I kept this up for many years, supplementing what I made on commissioned illustrations and paintings.

While airbrushing at the beach, an opening came up for an adjunct instructor for the airbrush class in the fine arts department at the local community college. I was a qualified applicant with a B.F.A. at that time. I had always enjoyed teaching, and this was a great opportunity. While at the college I continued my education, commuting two hours to Florida State University in Tallahassee where I received my M.F.A. I was then qualified to teach other art courses—which I did until I moved earlier this year.

An artist has to constantly be on the lookout for opportunities and be aware of current trends and the market.

What is a typical day like for you?

A freelance artist has to be self-motivated. You are the boss. You make the rules. I originally started teaching to fill in the off-season, but teaching became more important to me as time went on. Soon I found I was falling into the art teacher trap, where teaching takes away from studio time and you soon find you're not making art. Time for the studio has to be set aside.

My current studio is in my home or, rather, split between my garage and a room in the house. I get up every morning just like someone leaving to go to work, shower, get dressed, and go to the "studio." You have to forget the old cliché about "the artist's mood"; there's no such thing. It's a response to habit. You must develop the habit of creativity and just do it.

But you have to be ready to drop everything at a moment's notice and respond when an opportunity comes along. For example, one Thursday afternoon while in my studio painting, I received a phone call from a TV news station in Atlanta. A federal trial from Atlanta had a change of venue due to publicity and was being moved to the federal courthouse in Panama City, Florida, where I lived at the time.

They needed a courtroom artist and the local art center where I did volunteer work had given them my name (did I mention it helps to be active in the community?).

Of course I had never been in a courtroom and told them so up front. But I taught figure drawing and painted portraits. I offered to send them a portfolio (you should always have one ready to mail). However, because the trial was begining the following Monday, they asked me to fax them something immediately so they could make their decision. I got them to wait until the next day. I then researched my own library of illustration books and art magazines, found articles on courtroom artists, and spent the evening watching *Court TV* and sketching from the screen. I faxed them the work the next day and was in court sketching on Monday! Now my resume includes courtroom artist experience.

How does your career differ from that of a commercial artist?

Any art career has the same stresses that a "regular" job has, but commercial artists (illustrators, designers) have to meet deadlines—deadlines often set by people who wait till the last minute to hire you for the job. I remember responding to ads for illustration jobs and asking when would be a good time to come by. The answer was usually the same. "It doesn't matter. Any time is a good time. We're here from 9 A.M. until 3 A.M. or until the job is done."

They were serious. Go to any college campus and drive by the art building any time day or night. The lights are always on with students meeting deadlines. The same goes for any design firm. They're always there.

What do you like most about your job?

The thing I like most is that I get to use my talent every day. I get to create and pick and choose what I want to do. I set my hours to some extent and get a lot of satisfaction out of my work, since I see it from concept to completion. And I don't have to wear a tie to work!

What do you like least?

What I like least is the fact that there never seems to be an off day. Any day could be a day in the studio—and since it's at home, it's as though I never leave work.

Another drawback is that all arts and crafts shows are on weekends, so your weekends are tied up. When I was a T-shirt artist I worked seven days a week in the summertime. I went for seventeen years without taking Memorial Day, the Fourth of July, or Labor Day weekends off. Everyone else's holidays are your workdays.

The toughest part about claiming art as a career is earning respect. People respect your talent, but it stops there. They don't see you as a real worker, even if you happen to earn a better living than they do. And anyone who works at home will tell you that you don't get the same respect as a person in an office. No one would impose upon someone leaving to go to a building from nine to five like they would upon someone who is, presumably, hanging around the house all day.

What strategies can you recommend to artists concerning their portfolios?

As a full-time artist you must have several portfolios, one for each of your different artist lives. I have one of my fine art for the galleries, and one of my courtroom sketches for the media. Another portfolio contains illustrations and computer art for businesses and publishers. When I was a T-shirt artist I had a separate portfolio for that as well. You can't mix them. You must be many things, but keep them separate. In other words, you have to be a master of marketing.

For more advice concerning portfolios, I recommend the book *The Business of Art* and *Art Calendar* magazine, by Lee Caplin, published by Prentice-Hall in cooperation with the National Endowment for the Arts. Another good book is *The Artists' Survival Manual* by Toby Judith Klayman, published by Scribner's.

What general advice would you give to others considering this field?

Someone once said about creative processes, "If you *can* quit, quit"—meaning if it is possible for you to conceive of quitting a creative process, then it's not for you. You become an artist because you can't imagine doing anything else.

Art is not the field to go into for the money. You do it out of passion, even if it means doing something else to support it.

It's an extremely competitive field. Only the best and the most hardworking survive. It is not the myth that TV and the movies portray. In New York City alone there are 30,000 practicing artists, and there are jobs for only a fraction of those.

Before you decide on any career, pick the city where you would like to live and get the job section from their paper. Start researching the jobs available and look at the different fields. See how many art jobs are there. Start doing this before and during your studies.

So many times I've had young students going into art because they envision fame, glamour, and money. I've had older students coming back to college for a second career and picking art when they have a family to support and I'm very honest with them about the potential for disaster. The statistics are out there for you to research, but I've seen the evidence firsthand. The majority of art majors end up back in college to learn a new field. However, on the bright side, they will always have their talent, their creativity, and their art to enrich their personal lives.

To those who have made the decision to pursue a career in art, the best advice I can give you is to get yourself involved in the local art community. This is where you network and get noticed. Enter every show you can. Otherwise you're an isolated individual hunkered down in a studio somewhere. If it weren't for my volunteering at the local art center, I wouldn't have had half of the opportunities I've had.

Another thing is very important: So many times I've heard either artists or their parents claim that they are so talented that they don't need to take lessons or go to school. I had some of those illusions myself at first, but there is *no* substitute for the training you will get while studying in a university art program. And if you don't care for college, at least get training at one of the many art institutes around.

Looking at myself before and after my education, I can only say that it was money well spent. A degree is something no one can ever take from you.

I've had the opportunity to change streams many times, but I can't conceive of it. I love art and love making it—even in the lean times.

Financially, you get out of it what you put into it. As a freelancer there is no regular paycheck. No retirement plan other than your own. No Christmas bonus or sick leave. No insurance or other fringe benefits. You have to be frugal and learn to save, something I didn't realize in the early years.

Edwin Ryan Bailey is a self-employed artist in Winter Haven, Florida. He has been a professional artist since 1979. He earned his B.F.A. degree in illustration and design from Auburn University in Alabama in 1985 and his M.F.A. in studio art from Florida State University in Tallahassee in 1991.

INTERVIEW

Jim Anderson
Stained-Glass Artist

How did you get started in this field?

I started drawing and painting when I was young; even in my baby book it says stuff like "Jimmy is creative, Jimmy is artistic, Jimmy can draw." It's one of the areas where I got affirmation as a child.

I found that I really loved the combination of art and architecture, as opposed to paintings that just hang on walls. I liked the fact that stained glass becomes a permanent part of a building—it becomes architectural art.

My designs range to all kinds of styles—traditional as well as contemporary. I do hand-painted glass like you see in churches, and I do styles from different periods—Victorian, Federal, Edwardian, all periods.

Even as a kid I remember looking at church windows—just staring at them when I was in church. Little did I know that I'd be making them when I got older. I did my first church when I was twenty-six, St. George's Greek Orthodox Church in Hyannis. Now I'm amazed at that kind of undertaking for such a young man. I remember that my colleagues in New York and other places were astounded that the commission for a church was given to such a young artist.

After the Boston Museum School, I went to the Massachusetts College of Art to pursue a teaching certificate. I was afraid I wouldn't be able to support myself as an artist and I wanted something to fall back on. But during that time, I realized that I was already actually supporting myself. I started making windows for people and it paid my way through school.

Commissions started coming because people saw the work I did on my own house. I own a brownstone in the South End, which is the largest Victorian neighborhood in America with over 2,000 structures intact, bowfronts and brownstones.

I set up a workshop on the ground level of the townhouse so I'd have a place to work, then I did my doorways first. Other neighbors saw them and really loved them. Some of my neighbors were professional architects and they asked if I'd do their doors. Then other people saw the work and it mushroomed. Over the years I've done ten or fifteen doors on my street alone, and then other people on different streets started seeing them and hiring me.

Then, before I knew it, someone wrote an article about me in the *Boston Globe*, then articles appeared in other papers, then Channel Two did a documentary on revitalizing an old art form that included my work. At that point I started getting more and more work. I moved my studio out of my house to a more visible commercial area. I wanted to be able to keep my work on display in the windows.

Now I have a couple of assistants, one to help me, one to do repair and restoration work. How many assistants I have depends on the economy and how much work I have. As things improve I take on assistants, but if things drop off, I have to let them go. I always make sure there's enough work for at least myself, but now it's doing well, so I can afford to hire help.

I like going to people's houses and making beautiful windows they really love and that I feel are appropriate for their homes. I wouldn't put a modern window in a Victorian, for example—it wouldn't be suitable.

I meet a lot of interesting people in my work. Maybe it's because it's an unusual art form and it's usually interesting people who want it.

The work is fun and challenging and I'm always learning something new. The older I get, the more complicated and sophisticated the commissions get.

How would you describe your financial situation?

Money doesn't come in regularly, but it always seems to come in. Sometimes in big chunks, sometimes in little chunks. I never know when or what, but I haven't starved and I've always been able to pay my bills.

What advice would you offer to someone considering a career like yours?

Follow your dream; listen to your gut on what to do. Visualize what you want for yourself, then slowly go toward it.

But start slowly. In my first studio, I made worktables out of plywood and other basic, simple things I could find. Nothing fancy or expensive, whatever I could scavenge. I've refined the space over time.

Don't spend too much as you go along; let your business build up and don't overextend yourself.

How important the location of your studio is depends on the art form. If you're a painter, your aim is to be shown in galleries, so it doesn't matter so much where your studio is. But for other art forms, such as stained glass, it would.

There are cooperative buildings for artists in lots of major cities now. It's nice to work around other artists and share old warehouse space. It gives you a lot of exposure, plus it keeps you in the art community and the rents are usually reasonable.

Just work hard and keep an eye on every aspect of the business, including the bookkeeping.

Over the last twenty years, **Jim Anderson** has established himself as a successful stained-glass artist in Boston. His studio on Tremont Street in the revitalized South End neighborhood is called Anderson Glass Arts. He attended the Boston Museum School of Fine Arts and the Massachusetts College of Art, graduating with a B.F.A. and a teaching certificate.

EMPLOYMENT SETTINGS

Although most fine artists are usually self-employed and work in their own studios, they still depend on stores, galleries, museums, and private collectors as an outlet for their work. Others have what many consider to be the ideal situation—a combined working studio and storefront. Still others follow the art fair circuit: they pack up their artwork and tour the country on a regular basis, deriving most (if not all) of their income from this source alone.

However, many artists will tell you that any of these options can be risky, with no guarantee of sales. The art fair circuit, in particular, can be unreliable, vulnerable to the vagaries of the weather and the whim of impulse buyers or true art lovers and collectors.

For those who prefer the stability of job security and a dependable income, there is another setting in which artists and artisans may perform their art while being gainfully employed, either in a full- or part-time capacity.

LIVING HISTORY MUSEUMS

A living history museum is a vibrant, active village, town, or city where the day-to-day life of a particular time period has been authentically re-created. Colonial Williamsburg in Virginia and Plimoth Plantation in Massachusetts are just two examples of living history museums. Once you step through their gates, you leave the present behind. The houses and public buildings are restored originals or thoroughly researched reproductions. Interiors are outfitted with period furniture, cookware, bed linens, and tablecloths. Peek under a bed and you might even find a two- or three-hundred-year-old mousetrap.

Residents wear the clothing of their day and discuss their dreams and concerns with visitors as they go about their daily tasks. If you were to stop a costumed gentleman passing by and ask where the nearest McDonald's is, he wouldn't have any idea what you were talking about—unless he thought to direct you to a neighbor's farm. He might even do so using the dialect of his home country.

These large enterprises offer employment for professional and entry-level workers in a wide variety of categories. Those positions of particular interest to artists are artisans in the historic trades.

Artisans

Most living history museums employ skilled artisans to demonstrate early crafts and trades. Some of these artisans perform in the first-person, playing the role of a particular character of the time. Others wear twentieth-century clothing and discuss their craft from a modern perspective.

In the stores and workshops lining the Duke of Gloucester and Francis Streets in Colonial Williamsburg, you will find harness makers, milliners, tailors, needleworkers, silversmiths, apothecaries, candle makers, bookbinders, printers, and wig makers. In the Pilgrim Village and Crafts Center at Plimoth Plantation are coopers, blacksmiths, joiners (cabinetmakers), potters, basket makers, and weavers.

In addition to demonstrations, artisans often produce many of the items used on display in the various exhibits. This includes the furniture, cookware, and even sometimes the actual buildings.

Job Strategies for Living History Museums

The competition is fairly high for artisan or costumer positions at a living history museum. For example, the wardrobe department at Plimoth Plantation is a small one, currently employing only four workers. Other larger living history museums, such as Colonial Williamsburg, employ more people. A good way to get a foot in the door is to apply for an apprenticeship, internship, or work-study position. Many start out as character interpreters or presenters, then move into their chosen positions when openings occur.

INTERVIEW

Deb Mason
Potter

In the Crafts Center at Plimoth Plantation, four different potters demonstrate the art of seventeenth-century throwing techniques, though only one potter is on duty at a time. They also make all the pieces that are used in the village by the character interpreters. During the winter months when the museum is closed to visitors, the potters make enough items to replenish their stock.

In addition to her own home studio, where she teaches pottery classes, does commission work, and makes pieces for display at various galleries, Deb Mason spends two eight-hour days a week in the Crafts Center and supervises the other potters.

Tell us about your job in the Crafts Center.

In the Crafts Center we don't claim to be seventeenth-century people because pottery wasn't done in the village in 1627. But because of this, we have an advantage. We can talk to visitors in a way that's totally different from the interpreters. A visitor might go to the village, then come back to the Crafts Center to ask a question that the seventeenth-century interpreters couldn't answer. The interpreters have to speak as though they are pilgrims. They wouldn't have any knowledge beyond 1627.

For now we are working with twentieth-century equipment, though we are discussing the possibility of going back in time, using a kick wheel and a wood-burning stove. The electric wheels we use now might make throwing look faster and easier than it was in the seventeenth century, but the techniques are still very much the same.

The difference is we have to make only period pieces and that is where some of the difficulties come in. For example, we're trying to find the right clay bodies to work with. We have a few original pieces on display to study, and you can see the clay color and texture. We've been experimenting, trying to develop clay bodies that are close to the original.

That's been fairly successful, but we're having a tough time with glazes. They used a lot of lead back then. In fact, most every glaze was lead-based. Because we sell the pieces we make in the gift shop and they're also used in the village every day, we've been trying to get away from lead. It's hard to come up with glazes that have the same shine and the same colors; lead has a very typical look. We're using a ground glass that melts at a low temperature, which is a characteristic of lead and produces similar results.

We make ointment pots that the pilgrims used to hold salves and other healing lotions, apothecary jars, bowls, porringers for porridge, oil lamps, candlesticks, and pipkins, little cooking pots with a side handle and three little legs on the bottom. We also make a lot of three-handled cups. Pilgrims usually shared their eating implements. The cups are funny-looking things—a popular item in the craft shop.

Back then the pottery was hastily thrown. There's a real earthy quality to the pieces. Their perception of what was beautiful and what was utilitarian was different. What they strove for was extremely rough by today's standards.

My biggest problem is remembering not to throw too well. The advantage to that, though, for potters wanting to work here is that a high degree of skill is not necessary.

Deb Mason earned her B.A. in art with a major in ceramics in 1973 from Bennington College in Vermont. She taught ceramics full-time for thirteen years at a private school, and she was the head of the art department her last few years there. She joined the staff at Plimoth Plantation in 1992.

THE QUALIFICATIONS YOU'LL NEED

In the fine arts field, formal training requirements do not exist, but it is very difficult to become skilled enough to make a living without some basic training. Bachelor's and graduate degree programs in fine arts are offered in many colleges and universities. (See the introduction to this book for some samplings of art programs.)

In addition to the skills they learn or hone, art majors make important contacts during their formal training years. Instructors are often working artists with hands-on experience and advice to offer.

CAREER OUTLOOK

The fine arts field has a glamorous and exciting image. Many people with a love for drawing and creative ability qualify for entry to this field. As a result, competition is keen for both salaried jobs and freelance work in the fine arts.

However, employment of fine artists is expected to grow because of population growth, rising incomes, and increases in the number of people who appreciate fine arts.

Despite the expected employment growth, the numbers of those seeking entry to this field will continue to exceed employment opportunities. Fine artists, in particular, may find it difficult to earn a living solely by selling their artwork. Nonetheless, graphic arts studios, clients, and galleries alike are always on the lookout for artists who display outstanding talent, creativity, and style. Talented artists who have developed a mastery of artistic techniques and skills should continue to be in great demand.

INCOME

The gallery and artist predetermine how much each earns from a sale. Only the most successful fine artists are able to support themselves exclusively through the sale of their works, however. Most fine artists hold other jobs as well.

Earnings for self-employed visual artists vary widely. Those struggling to gain experience and a reputation may be forced to charge what amounts to less than the minimum wage for their work. Well-established fine artists may earn much more than salaried artists, but self-employed artists do not receive benefits such as paid holidays, sick leave, health insurance, or pensions.

Salaries for artisans within living history museums differ depending on whether they are full-time or part-time. The latter group earns an hourly wage ranging between $7.50 and $10. A new graduate just starting out full-time can expect to earn an annual salary in the high teens to mid-twenties, depending on the location and available funding.

In 1996, median earnings for salaried visual artists who usually work full-time were about $27,100 a year. The middle 50 percent earned between $20,000 and $36,400 a year. The top 10 percent earned more than $43,000, and the bottom 10 percent earned less than $15,000.

ART EDUCATION

The old adage, "Those who can, do; those who can't, teach," couldn't be farther from the truth for this particular career track. For the most part, art educators can *do* as well as teach.

For many, a job as an art teacher is a means to an end. They place their teaching job in a companion role to a parallel or primary career as a studio or commercial artist. The teaching job provides the security of a regular paycheck and health benefits that a freelancing career might not offer—at least not yet. Most states have tenure laws that prevent schoolteachers from being fired without just cause and due process. Teachers may obtain tenure after they have satisfactorily completed a probationary period of teaching, normally three years. Tenure is not a guarantee of a job, but it does provide some security.

Full-time art teaching positions in public or private schools are often on ten-month contracts, leaving summers and several weeks during the year free to pursue individual projects. There are also many settings where art teachers can work part-time, leaving even more hours free for studio or commercial art undertakings.

For others, teaching is the end to the means. For these teachers, a love of and skill in the subject area is best expressed by sharing it and encouraging it in others. Although most probably still practice their art, they do it more for self-expression and self-satisfaction than as a way to earn a living.

Some would say that all artists are able to teach, that the ability to share technique and encourage proficiency is a natural extension of their own creativity. This may or may not be true.

However, no matter the subject area—art or science or air-conditioning repair—there are certain qualities and skills that all teachers must possess in addition to being knowledgeable about their specialty. The ability to communicate, inspire trust and confidence, and motivate students, as well as understand their educational and emotional needs, is essential for teachers. Instructors also should be organized, dependable, and patient, as well as creative.

THE QUALIFICATIONS YOU'LL NEED

Is it necessary to have a college degree to teach art? The answer to that is a resounding "no." The degree of formal training and qualifications varies depending on the work setting. In many instructional situations and settings, an artist's skill, as evidenced by his or her portfolio or reputation, is highly sought after. Professional artists who lack a formal degree but have made a name for themselves are often invited as guest lecturers to teach studio classes or workshops at various art schools or other settings across the country. But this opportunity is usually available only for established artists. However, those who have not yet earned a reputation can still find employment without the degree. This employment is generally limited to part-time positions, though, usually with an hourly wage for a salary.

For full-time positions with professional-level salaries, a bachelor's degree is the usual minimum requirement. But is it necessary to have a state teaching certificate to find work as an art teacher? To work in most public school systems, the answer to that question is "yes"—although some public school districts make provisions to grant temporary certification to noncredentialed teachers. These districts have had difficultly securing teachers because of location or pay scale. However, this practice is not common.

Some private schools will also hire noncertified teachers, but with the high supply and relatively small demand for art teachers, they, too, often require teachers to have the same credentials as the public schools do.

To work in most public school systems, a bachelor's degree with a teaching certification is required. In other settings, such as art schools and colleges, community colleges, and four-year universities, postgraduate degrees are required. The following paragraphs offer a detailed look at the different educational settings and their requirements.

Kindergarten and Elementary

Traditional education programs for kindergarten and elementary-school teachers include courses designed specifically for those preparing to teach a particular subject area, such as art, music, or mathematics, as well as prescribed professional education courses, such as the philosophy of education, the psychology of learning, and teaching methods.

Secondary

Aspiring secondary-school art teachers either major in art while also taking education courses, or major in education and take art courses.

Alternative Teacher Certification Many states offer alternative teacher certification programs for people who have college training in the subject they will teach but do not have the necessary education courses required for a regular certificate. Alternative certification programs were originally designed to ease teacher shortages in certain subjects, such as mathematics and science. The programs have expanded to attract other people to teaching, including recent college graduates and midcareer changers.

In some programs, individuals begin teaching immediately under provisional certification. They must work under the close supervision of experienced educators for one or two years while taking education courses outside school hours; if they progress satisfactorily, they will receive regular certification.

Under other programs, college graduates who do not meet certification requirements take only those courses that they lack, and then become certified. This may require one or two semesters of full-time study.

Aspiring teachers who need certification may also enter programs that grant a master's degree in education as well as certification. States also issue emergency certificates to individuals who do not meet all the requirements for a regular certificate when schools cannot hire enough certified teachers.

Competency Testing Almost all states require applicants for teacher certification to be tested for competency in basic reading, writing, math, and teaching skills, as well as subject matter proficiency. Almost all states require continuing education for renewal of the teacher's certificate, and some require a master's degree.

Reciprocity Many states have reciprocity agreements that make it easier for teachers certified in one state to become certified in another. Teachers may become board certified by successfully completing the National Board for Professional Teaching Standards certification process. This certification is voluntary but may result in a higher salary.

Information on certification requirements and approved teacher training institutions is available from local school systems and state departments of education.

Colleges and Universities

Most college and university faculty are classified according to four academic ranks: professor, associate professor, assistant professor, and instructor. A small number are lecturers.

Most faculty members are hired as instructors or assistant professors. Four-year colleges and universities generally hire doctoral degree holders for full-time, tenure-track positions, but may hire master's degree holders or doctoral candidates for certain disciplines, such as the arts, or for part-time and temporary jobs.

Doctoral programs usually require four to seven years of full-time study beyond the bachelor's degree. Most candidates specialize in a subfield of a discipline—for example, European art history—but also take courses covering the whole discipline. Programs include twenty or more increasingly specialized courses and seminars plus comprehensive examinations on all major areas of the field. They also include a dissertation, a book-length report on original research to answer some significant question in the field.

Students in the natural sciences and engineering usually do laboratory work; in the humanities, they study original documents and other published material. The dissertation, done under the guidance of one or more faculty advisors, usually requires one or two years of full-time work.

Adult Education   Training requirements vary widely by state and by subject. In general, teachers need work or other experience in their field, and some fields require a license or certificate for full professional status.

In some cases, particularly at educational institutions, a bachelor's, master's, or doctoral degree is required, especially to teach courses that students can apply toward a four-year degree program.

In other cases, an acceptable portfolio of work is required. For example, to secure a job teaching a flower-arranging course, an applicant would need to show examples of previous work.

Adult education teachers update their skills through continuing education to maintain certification requirements, which vary among institutions. Teachers may take part in seminars, conferences, or graduate courses in adult education, training and development, or human resources development.

Adult education teachers should communicate and relate well with adults, enjoy working with people, and be able to motivate their students.

GETTING AHEAD

With additional preparation and certification, teachers may become administrators or supervisors, although the number of positions is limited. In some systems, highly qualified, experienced teachers can become senior or mentor teachers, with higher pay and additional responsibilities. They guide and assist less experienced teachers while fulfilling most of their teaching responsibilities.

Some faculty—based on teaching experience, research, publication, and service on campus committees and task forces—move into administrative and managerial positions, such as departmental chair, dean, and president. At four-year institutions, such advancement requires a doctoral degree.

EMPLOYMENT SETTINGS

Art instructors have a variety of settings from which to choose. Working conditions, pay scales, and the attitude, motivation, and proficiency of the students will vary depending upon the setting. Here is a sampling of the possible avenues to pursue:

Adult education centers	Prisons
Alternative schools	Rehabilitation centers
Art schools	Group homes
Private schools	Halfway houses
Public schools	Summer camps
Community colleges	Recreation centers
Four-year colleges and universities	Parks departments

Religious organizations   Community centers

Museums   Discovery centers

International schools   Government organizations

WORKING CONDITIONS

Primary and Secondary Schools

Kindergarten and elementary-school teachers play a vital role in the development of children. What children learn and experience during their early years can shape their views of themselves and the world, and affect later success or failure in school, work, and their personal lives. Their early exposure to creating art also shapes how they will feel about their abilities when they reach adulthood. As many of us know, a negative experience can create the attitude, "I can't draw." The successful art teacher will know how to instill confidence in all her students, no matter their level of ability or natural talent.

Kindergarten and elementary-school teachers introduce children to numbers, language, science, social studies—and of course, art. They may use games, music, artwork, films, slides, computers, and other instructional technology to teach basic skills. When the focus is on art education, the kindergarten or elementary-school teacher uses a number of methods and different equipment to encourage student creativity. Young children work with crayons, pencils, and watercolors and create drawings and craft projects. Often the teacher will suggest the subject or theme for a drawing or painting or demonstrate a technique for a particular project such as a collage, pop-up, or clay pinch-pot. In most art rooms, teachers display their students' work on the walls and tables, creating a stimulating environment and a sense of pride for the students.

Most elementary-school teachers instruct one class of children in several subjects. In some schools, two or more teachers teach as a team and are jointly responsible for a group of students in at least one subject. In other schools, a teacher may teach one special subject—usually art, music, reading, science, arithmetic, or physical education—to a number of classes. A small but growing number of teachers instruct multilevel classrooms with students at several different learning levels.

As you will see from the interviews later in this chapter, art teachers work with different populations. They may have students with special educational needs—or students with severe discipline problems. In addition to classroom activities, which can involve back-to-back art classes with little time for breaks, art teachers have many of the same duties as general classroom teachers. They plan and evaluate lessons, sometimes in collaboration with teachers of related subjects. They also prepare tests, grade papers, prepare report cards, oversee study halls and homerooms, supervise extracurricular activities, and meet with parents and school staff to discuss a student's academic progress or personal problems. In many schools, teachers help make decisions regarding the budget, personnel, textbook choices, curriculum design, and teaching methods.

Secondary-school teachers help students delve more deeply into subjects introduced in elementary school and learn more about the world and about themselves. They specialize in a specific subject, such as art, music, English,

Spanish, mathematics, history, or biology. Art teachers may teach a variety of related courses, such as line drawing, oil painting, pottery, and art history.

Secondary-school teachers may assist a student in choosing courses, colleges, and careers. Art teachers with students wanting to pursue either the fine arts or commercial arts as a career should be familiar with choices for further education.

Teachers design their classroom presentations to meet student needs and abilities, often following the art curriculum established by the school board. They also may work with students individually. Teachers assign lessons, give tests, hear oral presentations, and maintain classroom discipline.

Teachers observe and evaluate a student's performance and potential. Teachers are increasingly using new assessment methods, such as examining a portfolio of a student's artwork to measure student achievement. Teachers assess the portfolio at the end of a learning period to judge a student's overall progress. They may then provide additional assistance in areas where a student may need help.

Seeing students develop new skills and gain an appreciation for art and the study of art can be very rewarding.

Art Schools, Colleges, and Universities

Faculty are generally organized into departments or divisions, based on subject or field. They usually teach several different courses in their department; for example, in a B.F.A. program, an art instructor might teach courses in oil painting, pastels, and watercolors. They may instruct undergraduate or graduate students, or both.

In art schools or colleges faculty may work with small groups in studio classes or give lectures on art history or other areas to several hundred students in large halls. They also grade and evaluate assignments and projects and advise and work with students individually. In universities, they also counsel, advise, teach, and supervise graduate student research.

Most faculty members serve on academic or administrative committees that deal with the policies of their institution, departmental matters, academic issues, curricula, budgets, equipment purchases, and hiring. Some work with student organizations. Department heads generally have heavier administrative responsibilities.

The amount of time spent on each of these activities varies by individual circumstance and type of institution. Faculty members at universities generally spend a significant part of their time doing research; those in four-year colleges, somewhat less; and those in two-year colleges, relatively little. However, the teaching load usually is heavier in two-year colleges.

College faculty generally have flexible schedules. They must be present for classes, usually twelve to sixteen hours a week, and for faculty and committee meetings. Most establish regular office hours for student consultations, usually three to six hours per week. Otherwise, they are relatively free to decide when and where they will work, and how much time to devote to course preparation, evaluating student progress, studio work, and other activities.

They may work staggered hours and teach classes at night and on weekends, particularly those faculty who teach older students who may have full-time jobs or family responsibilities on weekdays. They have even greater flexibility during the summer and school holidays, when they may teach, do their own artwork, travel, or pursue nonacademic interests.

Adult Education

Art teachers working in adult education have a variety of settings from which to choose. They are employed by public school systems; community and junior colleges; universities; businesses that provide formal education and training for their employees; art and photography schools and institutes; job training centers; community organizations; recreational facilities such as the YMCA; and religious organizations such as neighborhood Jewish Community Centers.

Many adult education teachers work part-time. To accommodate students who may have jobs or family responsibilities, many courses are offered at night or on weekends and range from two- to four-hour workshops and one-day mini-sessions to semester-long courses.

Since adult education teachers work with adult students, they do not encounter some of the behavioral or social problems sometimes found when teaching younger students. The adults are there by choice and are usually highly motivated—attributes that can make teaching these art students rewarding and satisfying.

THE JOB HUNT

College Career Placement Centers

Check with your college career office. Career offices regularly receive notices of job openings. You can also leave your resume on file there. Prospective employers regularly contact college career offices looking for likely candidates.

Help Wanted Ads

Read the newspapers from your area or from the geographic location in which you'd prefer to work. A trip to the library will reveal periodicals you might not have been aware of—and will be less of a burden on your budget.

The Internet

This is an incredible source for job hunting. Use any of the search engines available to you and type in key words such as *employment*, *art*, *teaching*, and *jobs*. You will discover a wealth of information on-line: organizations, educational institutions, publications, and a wide variety of potential employers and job search services, most of which are available to you at no charge except for Internet provider service fees. Most public libraries now offer free Internet access as well.

Internships and Volunteering

Art educators, especially those hoping to land a museum job, will find internships and volunteering stints to be the most important ways to launch their careers. Museums cry out for volunteer help, and internships can be arranged through your university. Once in the door, make yourself indispensable. When a job opening occurs, you'll be there on the spot, ready to step in. (You can read more about museum work in Chapter 5.)

Direct Contact

Walk inside, set your portfolio or resume down on the appropriate desk, and you might just land yourself a job. This approach works best in adult education centers, community centers, and other related settings (see the list under "Employment Settings" earlier in this chapter).

The Chronicle of Higher Education

This is the old standby for those seeking positions within two- and four-year colleges and universities. It is a weekly publication available by subscription, in any library, or at your college placement office.

Placement Agencies

For private schools particularly, both in the United States and abroad, placement agencies can provide a valuable source for finding employment. Some charge either the employer or the prospective employee a fee; others charge both.

CAREER OUTLOOK

Primary and Secondary Schools

The job market for teachers varies widely by geographic area and by subject specialty. Many inner cities (characterized by high crime rates, high poverty rates, and overcrowded conditions) and rural areas (characterized by remote location and relatively low salaries) have difficulty attracting enough teachers, so job prospects should continue to be better in these areas than in suburban districts.

Currently, many school districts have difficulty hiring qualified teachers in some subjects—mathematics, science (especially chemistry and physics), bilingual education, and computer science. Specialties that currently have an abundance of qualified teachers include art, general elementary education, English, physical education, and social studies. As a result, art teachers face stiffer competition locating a job. Art teachers who are geographically mobile and who obtain licensure in more than one subject should have a distinct advantage.

With enrollments of minorities increasing, coupled with a shortage of minority teachers, efforts to recruit minority teachers should intensify. Also, the number of non–English speaking students has grown dramatically (especially in California and Florida, which have large Spanish-speaking student populations), creating demand for bilingual teachers and those who teach English as a second language (ESL).

Overall employment of kindergarten, elementary-school, and secondary-school teachers is expected to increase about as fast as the average for all occupations through the year 2006. The expected retirement of a large number of teachers currently in their forties and fifties should open up many additional jobs. However, projected employment growth varies among individual teaching occupations.

Employment of secondary-school teachers is expected to grow faster than the average for all occupations through the year 2006, while average employment growth is projected for kindergarten and elementary-school teachers. Assuming relatively little change in average class size, employment growth of teachers depends on population growth rates and corresponding student enrollments. Enrollment of fourteen- to seventeen-year-olds is expected to grow through the year 2006. Enrollment of five- to thirteen-year-olds is also projected to increase, but at a slower rate through the year 2002, and then decline.

The number of teachers employed is also dependent on state and local expenditures for education. Pressures from taxpayers to limit spending could result in fewer teachers than projected; pressures to spend more to improve the quality of education could increase the teacher workforce.

The supply of teachers also is expected to increase in response to reports of improved job prospects, more teacher involvement in school policy, and greater public interest in education. In recent years, the total number of bachelor's and master's degrees granted in education has steadily increased. In addition, more teachers will be drawn from a reserve pool of career changers, substitute teachers, and teachers completing alternative certification programs, relocating to different schools, and reentering the workforce.

Higher Education   Employment of college and university faculty is expected to increase about as fast as the average for all occupations through the year 2006 as enrollments in higher education increase. Many additional openings will arise as faculty members retire. Faculty retirements should increase significantly through 2006 as a large number of faculty who entered the profession during the 1950s and 1960s reach retirement age. Most faculty members likely to retire are full-time tenured professors. However, in an effort to cut costs, some institutions are expected to either leave these positions vacant or hire part-time, nontenured faculty as replacements.

Prospective job applicants should be prepared to face keen competition for available jobs as growing numbers of Ph.D. graduates, including foreign-born doctoral degree holders, vie for fewer full-time openings. As more and more applicants with doctoral degrees compete for openings, master's degree holders may find competition for jobs even more intense.

Enrollments in institutions of higher education increased in the mid-1980s through the early 1990s despite a decline in the traditional college-age (eighteen to twenty-four) population. This resulted from a growing number of part-time, female, and older students. Between 1996 and 2006, the traditional college-age population will begin to grow again, spurred by the leading edge of the baby-boom "echo" generation (children of the baby boomers) reaching college age. College enrollment is projected to rise from fourteen million in 1996 to sixteen million in 2006, an increase of 14 percent.

In the past two decades, keen competition for faculty jobs forced some applicants to accept part-time or short-term academic appointments that offered little hope of tenure, and others to seek nonacademic positions. This trend of hiring adjunct or part-time faculty is likely to continue due to financial difficulties faced by colleges and universities. Many colleges, faced with reduced state funding for higher education, have increased the hiring of part-time faculty to save money on pay and benefits. Public two-year colleges employ a significantly higher number of part-time faculty as a percentage of their total staff than public four-year colleges and universities, but all institutions have increased their part-time hiring. With uncertainty over future funding, many colleges and universities are continuing to cut costs by eliminating some academic programs, increasing class size, and closely monitoring all expenses.

As enrollments and retirements start increasing at a faster pace, opportunities for college faculty may begin to improve somewhat. Growing numbers of students will necessitate hiring more faculty to teach. At the same time, many faculty will be retiring, opening up even more positions. Job prospects will continue to be better in certain fields—business, engineering, health science, and computer science, for example—that offer attractive nonacademic job opportunities and attract fewer applicants for academic positions.

Employment of college faculty is affected by the nonacademic job market. Excellent job prospects in a field—for example, computer science from the late 1970s to the mid-1980s—cause more students to enroll, increasing faculty needs in that field. On the other hand, poor job prospects in a field, such as art in recent years, discourages students and reduces demand for faculty.

Adult Education

Employment of adult education teachers is expected to grow faster than the average for all occupations through 2006 as the demand for adult education programs continues to rise. Opportunities should be best for part-time positions. An estimated four out of ten adults participate in some form of adult education. Participation in continuing education grows as the educational attainment of the population increases. Both employers and employees are realizing that lifelong learning is important for success. An increasing number of adults are participating in classes for personal enrichment and enjoyment. Art and art-related courses have always proved popular at the adult education level. Funding is usually provided through registration fees, and art classes can often have waiting lists of people wanting to sign up.

Additional job openings for adult education teachers will stem from the need to replace persons who leave the occupation. Many teach part-time and move into and out of the occupation for other jobs, due to family responsibilities, or to retire.

EARNINGS

School Systems

According to the National Education Association, the estimated average salary of all public elementary- and secondary-school teachers in the 1995–96 school year was $37,900. Public secondary-school teachers averaged about $38,600 a year, while public elementary-school teachers averaged $37,300. Private-school teachers generally earn less than public school teachers.

In 1996, over half of all public-school teachers belonged to unions—mainly the American Federation of Teachers and the National Education Association—that bargain with school systems over wages, hours, and the terms and conditions of employment.

In some schools, teachers receive extra pay for coaching sports and working with students in extracurricular activities. Some teachers earn extra income during the summer working in the school system or in other jobs.

Higher Education   Earnings vary according to faculty rank and type of institution, geographic area, and field. According to a survey by the American Association of University Professors, salaries for full-time faculty currently average $51,000. By rank, the average for professors is $65,400; associate professors, $48,300; assistant professors, $40,100; instructors, $30,800; and lecturers, $33,700.

Faculty in four-year institutions earn higher salaries, on the average, than those in two-year schools. Average salaries for faculty in public institutions ($50,400) are lower than those for private independent institutions ($57,500) but higher than those for religion-affiliated private institutions ($45,200).

In fields with high-paying nonacademic alternatives—notably medicine and law but also engineering and business, among others—earnings exceed these averages. In others—such as the humanities and education—they are lower.

Most faculty members have significant earnings in addition to their base salary, from consulting, teaching additional courses, research, writing for publication, or other employment, both during the academic year and the summer.

Most college and university faculty enjoy some unique benefits, including access to campus facilities, tuition waivers for dependents, housing and travel allowances, and paid sabbatical leaves. Part-time faculty have fewer benefits than full-time faculty, and usually do not receive health insurance, retirement benefits, or sabbatical leave.

Adult Education   In 1996, salaried adult education teachers who usually worked full-time had median earnings around $31,300 a year. The middle 50 percent earned between $19,200 and $44,800. The lowest 10 percent earned about $13,100, while the top 10 percent earned more than $56,600.

Earnings varied widely by subject, academic credentials, experience, and region of the country. Part-time instructors generally are paid hourly and do not receive benefits or pay for preparation time outside of class.

INTERVIEW

Mindy Conley
Art Specialist, Grades K–4

How did you get started in this field?

I began teaching art classes to children at the Jewish Community Center in Savannah, Georgia, in 1989, while I was working on my M.F.A. at Savannah College of Art and Design. I did one year of the two-year M.F.A. program in fiber arts at Savannah College of Art and Design, but did not finish. In 1990, I returned to Nashville and lucked into a job at Cheekwood Fine Arts Center and Botanic Gardens. Here I combined my B.S. in early childhood education and art experience to do art outreach into public and private schools in the area. I also designed programs, taught children's and adult art classes, did a summer camp program, and managed the art studios.

I also directed an after-school care program at the Ensworth School, an affluent private school in Nashville, and developed and implemented a summer day-camp program for children five to eight years old, which was interdisciplinary but heavy on the arts.

In 1996 I took the position of director of art for a new private school for gifted children (K–8) that was starting in Nashville. But the school closed after the fall semester because the headmistress basically stole all of the money.

I started part-time in 1996 at my current school, then a year later became a full-time art specialist. A new core curriculum was adopted by the school board in Nashville and this put full-time art teachers in all of the schools. I had to take two classes to get an add-on endorsement from the state for K–12 art.

Basically, I entered the art teaching profession through the back door. I wanted to be a teacher. But upon graduation, I taught kindergarten for six months in a child-care setting and thought, "What am I doing?" I had always loved art but I had never considered it as a career choice. I decided to take some time and pursue some art classes. While working on my M.F.A., I realized that I could never support myself as a studio artist. But thanks to a good friend and some luck, I acquired a position at an art museum that combined my education and art background. Here I taught art outreach to children in public and private schools in the area and did teacher in-service training, among other things.

I first became a certified teacher and then added the art experience while pursuing the art field. When I needed the official art certification, it was just a matter of taking a few more classes.

What is your job like?

Sometimes I think I must be crazy. Why do I do this? But then I remember the good things. It is hard to express to people why you teach when there are some real drawbacks. But we just do. We have to.

Every day is different and full of unexpected surprises. A teacher has to be a flexible person. You have to do advance planning and then be ready to change it all. Our system mandates that each classroom teacher get one hour of uninterrupted planning time each day. So their uninterrupted planning time is while their students are at an hour of art, music, or PE.

It is our responsibility to switch the students between two specialists. Each school decides how to set up the schedule. But usually the specialists' planning time is not a full hour but split: some in the morning, some in the middle of the day, and some after school.

I arrive at 8:15 but do not begin teaching until 9:00 because of the morning routines that are conducted in the classrooms. I teach from 9:00 until 11:00 straight with no breaks between classes, a rotating door from one class to another.

I have lunch and planning from 11:00 until 12:00 and teach from 12:00 until 3:00. School dismisses at 3:20. This is when I do bus/dismissal duty (which all teachers do).

I spend the morning preparing materials, slides, or whatever I am using that day. We have to do a week's planning in advance and hand our lesson plans in the Friday before. But in art, you never know if students will progress through a project faster or slower than you expect so you are always revising your plans.

There are also times when a class may have a field trip or assembly that you didn't know about . . . remember, flexibility. If a class has an assembly during art, it is my responsibility to take them to this assembly. In education, unlike many professions, you are dealing with children, and this alone adds the element of greatest surprise. You never know what experiences these children are bringing to class that day. Some may be hungry and you get them food, some may be tired so you let them sleep, some may be angry or sad because of something that happened at home or earlier in the school day. All of these things affect the tone of the classroom, a student's ability to learn, and your ability to teach.

You have discipline problems that must be handled immediately and often take you away from teaching the whole class. Bottom line, you meet your students' physical and emotional needs first and teach art second.

Fortunately, most students love to come to art class. It's a great opportunity for many to succeed when they are experiencing failure in other areas. I believe it is inaccurate when people say you have to love children to teach. It's great if you do, but you must, must, must respect them first.

A good teacher should never find teaching boring. It is full of unexpected surprises such as the faculty meeting you swear you didn't know about, paperwork that was needed yesterday by your principal or art supervisor, a parent that drops in and must talk to you, a new student who arrives unexpectedly, or a student leaving who needs all of his artwork.

Being a part of a school faculty is like being a part of a family. You support each other, sometimes get on each other's nerves, share ideas, work together to support children, and often fight over the copy machine (when it is working). And most importantly, you interject humor whenever possible.

Teaching is not glamorous. You often work in old buildings or portable trailers, have limited adult bathrooms, deal with head lice and vomit, eat cafeteria food or bring your own, worry over a student, never have enough money for materials, sometimes spend your own money, deal with unhappy parents, do large amounts of paperwork. But the rewards are something that only a teacher can know. You get out of it what you put into it. Teaching is a profession . . . but it is also a calling.

What do you like the most about your job?

I love the content area that I teach. I can't imagine being in a self-contained classroom teaching the different academic subject areas. However, art is academic and so important to a child's full development. In art, you do production, but in a quality art program you also teach about art aesthetics, criticism, and history. Art can relate to those other content areas such as history, language, math, and even science. It is rewarding to expose children to a world they may never have been exposed to, to introduce them to art and artists from around the world, and to show them that there are so many ways for people to express themselves.

In art a child gets to express, create, and problem solve while also experiencing a variety of art media. It's fun! It involves all of our senses. And I enjoy teaching all of the students. I get to experience the special qualities of all of the different age levels. And I am rewarded personally by the diverse population that I serve.

In a public school setting, you generally have a population of students that have a wide variety of needs. You have good benefits and can become vested or tenured, which offers job security. (Our system has a four-year period for tenure. There are different requirements system to system for this. It involves observations by your principal, evaluations, and submitting a lesson and unit plan.)

What do you like the least?

The downside to teaching in a public school system, and possibly some private schools, is the paperwork and funding. Too much of the former and not enough of the latter. I love what I teach, but teaching is still a job that involves accountability, issues of testing and grading, faculty meetings, committee obligations, scheduling problems, discipline issues, and extra jobs such as bus duty.

Each school and school system is set up differently in regard to how they handle an art program. I worked for two years in a portable (outside trailer) with no bathroom or running water. When we painted, I carried buckets of water to a large trash can in the room. Cleaning tables and hands involved a lot of baby wipes. I now have a new portable with two bathrooms and sinks. I'm in heaven.

Art involves a lot of consumable materials. Funding can come from several different types of accounts. Some funds are for consumables and some are for nonconsumables. It's a paperwork nightmare figuring out what to buy with what and to budget wisely. Because when the money is gone, it is gone.

There is a wealth of art information on the Internet, but funding is hard to come by to put computers, phone lines, and modems in an art room. The arts have a long way to go with many administrators to get beyond being viewed as fluff, much less in need of technology. I am lucky to have a principal that supports the arts and helped me acquire a clay kiln. Our city also has a Pencil Partner program that hooks up businesses and corporations with schools. They have been a great source for materials support as well as mentoring in the classrooms. And there are always grants that we can apply for. But that involves more paperwork. Even the most organized teachers will find themselves working at home at times. That's the nature of the job if you want to do it well.

What kind of salary can someone in your position expect to earn?

I entered with a master's degree and four years of experience. My beginning pay in 1997 was $32,419. The pay has not come up yet because our teacher's union has been in negotiations with the board for a year and can't come up with a raise or a new contract.

Each state and school system within that state has its own pay scale. This information is available through the Board of Education or the Central Office. It can also be found on the Internet. I acquired my master's degree for the knowledge, of course, but to also raise my pay to the master's level.

What can you offer to prospective art teachers?

Visit elementary, middle, and high schools and talk to teachers there about what the students are like. You need to figure out what age you want to teach.

But while you are in school, cover your bases. For instance, I got my certification in early childhood education K–3, but wish I had done K–12.

Talk to the schools of your choice about how their programs are set up for art education. And when they are having you learn to write a lesson plan, don't think, "I've done this before" . . . do it again and again. You have to be able to do logical, organized planning.

When you do start teaching, always do a sample of a project before you do it with children. You need to be able to troubleshoot. And be willing to admit to yourself when a project is a flop, and go on.

Teaching art is a great job and can be very enjoyable. But go into it with your eyes open. If anyone pursues teaching art because they think it is an easy subject to teach, then they shouldn't become an art teacher. A quality art program should have substance and art teachers are accountable to their students for their learning like all other teachers. I was lucky to be trained in a teacher program that got us into classrooms and interacting with students early on. However, know that you can be trained in the best program and when you actually start teaching, you won't be totally prepared. But stick with it, and find a mentor.

A teacher needs to be organized. If it's not a personal characteristic of yours, that is OK. But know that it is something that you will constantly need to work on.

Teachers need to be problem solvers and resourceful. You need to be willing to tap into all kinds of resources for art materials. Scavenging is an art teacher's survival. Learn to look at things in a new way and gauge how they can be useful to you in your teaching. Find a parent volunteer, even if it is just one, and use them. They are great for getting the artwork hung in the hallways.

You should talk to other art teachers in a variety of teaching settings. Ask them about their discipline plan and classroom management techniques. These are two areas that universities can teach you in theory, but practicing teachers can actually give you practical advice.

Join professional organizations. I belong to the NAEA (National Art Education Association) and its Tennessee branch (TAEA).

Mindy Conley teaches art at Brookmeade Elementary School in Nashville, Tennessee. She has been teaching art to children and adults in different settings for ten years. She earned her B.S. in early childhood education from Vanderbilt University in Nashville in 1986 and her M.Ed. in curriculum and instruction from Trevecca Nazarene University, also in Nashville, in 1996. She recently started work on an Ed.D. at Trevecca Nazarene University.

INTERVIEW

Peggy Peters
Art Teacher

Tell us about your entrance into this field.

To get certified to teach in Texas is quite difficult. I had to complete thirty-six hours of college course work, though I already had a B.F.A., and pass a pre-entry exam to get into the education department, and pass a state battery of tests to get a teaching certificate.

Tell us about your job.

I am currently teaching in the San Antonio Independent School District as an art teacher at one of their alternative schools where students with criminal records (assault, drugs, gang affiliation, etc.), persistent behavior problems, and undiagnosed mental problems are placed.

Previously, I taught everything from elementary fine arts to fine arts in high school. I seem to usually get jobs with problem kids.

I teach three classes a day with from six to no more than eighteen students per class. Summers off, of course. No year-round school.

One of the reasons I teach is that because the percentage of people who succeed in the arts is very small, it was the logical choice for someone who wanted to use her talents on a daily basis. Also, as we teach only 183 days a year, with long breaks, it allows some leeway in doing individual work.

What is a typical day like for you?

My typical day at the alternative school is easier than at a regular school— this makes up for the danger to me. I report at 8:00 A.M. We sometimes have morning meetings or staffings with the counselor to explain problems that new students might have.

At 8:30 classes start. Classes are ninety minutes. I teach three a day and have one ninety-minute planning period and thirty minutes for lunch. Because this is an alternative school, I have to take special precautions to check the room before and after each class, to clean up and report any tagging or drug or gang signs students may have left. We had a riot in the cafeteria one day because of too many students in rival gangs, and our campus police officer and one teacher were hospitalized from student attacks this year.

Even so, it's easier than the last school at which I taught, where the behavior was just as bad and I had a horribly difficult class load. I know many artists who teach at alternative schools or in prisons or special schools. This seems to be the preferred type of teaching for many professional artists.

We get off work at 3:30 and, as I don't give homework, I usually have evenings free to do my own illustration work—if I have any energy, that is, depending on how difficult the day was. I also document problems and call parents at night if necessary.

What are the salaries like for teachers in your field?

You often hear how bad teaching salaries are—this is not true when you take into account that we teach only 183 days a year. In San Antonio teaching is one of the better paid professions. Also we get automatic raises each year, plus cost of living increases.

What are the downsides to teaching?

What no one is prepared for when entering teaching these days is how very difficult it has become because so many students are emotionally disturbed. We act as full-time social workers as well as teachers.

I started teaching nine years ago at a special school for overaged under-achievers, mostly Hispanic students with criminal records. I was chosen by the counselor because she understood what the arts could do for students. I was very successful.

I am noted for getting a remarkably high level of achievement from all of my students, mainly because I know how to teach technique—how to draw, how to see, how to think, how to plan. Art is not magic; mostly it's technique at a student level.

At the alternative school where I teach now, I work with students in grades six through twelve teaching basic art. As we get students in nine-week shifts, each starting on a different day, depending on when they were shipped off their home campus (for reasons ranging from assaulting teachers or students to getting caught with drugs, etc.), I have to teach them projects that they can start and stop at any time, using basic skills such as design, drawing, and execution.

I am limited in the materials I can use because I can't use things that the students will try to steal to do harm to themselves or others. India ink, for example, is used by some of the kids to rub into their skin, which they have scratched with a razor to make a kind of fuzzy but permanent tattoo.

Currently, I have to keep a very careful count on any markers or wax pencils I issue as we have a major problem with taggers who mark up buildings and do hundreds of thousands of dollars' worth of property damage around town. Their latest thing is to scratch their tags into glass windows and doors. This is permanent and cannot be removed. I had several students who did jail time for tagging and kept doing it regardless of the consequences.

You can be given unbelievable class loads. At the elementary school where I worked for one year, I taught art, music, drama, and dance to fifteen classes (340 students) and I was told I was lucky not to be teaching PE as well.

Teachers can be subjected to unbelievable stress. We have to deal with both overstressed fellow teachers who are frequently the victims of out-of-control administrators and a very high percentage of problem students. Mainstreaming of emotionally disturbed students means we can have three persistent misbehavior students, two emotionally disturbed students, four learning disabled students, two physically handicapped students, and any number of regular students in the same classroom. We have to justify our lesson plans with administration for each student and explain why we might have some students who are failing all their classes.

We are responsible for following a very complex set of guidelines to correct problem behavior in each student. We must counsel the student privately and document our conversation. We must get written contractual agreements with the student; we must reseat and reteach the student; we must refer students to their homeroom teacher, counselor, and home team to discuss the problem; we must chart their behavior during each class period; and we must call and document each behavior with parents—all before we can refer a student to an administrator for any behavior problem. And in the average classroom you will have many, many behavior problems.

In a poor school district, like the ones in which I teach, the parents are usually supportive but unable to control their children who are involved in gang activity. It is an unusual experience to try to correct the behavior of a student who you happen to know for a fact is engaged in nightly drive-by shooting activities. If we teachers really knew how dangerous students are we would not have the courage to deal with them.

An additional problem is that many schools are old and not maintained properly so the atmosphere is very polluted, causing health problems for teachers and students. I have been in schools where the air-conditioning system was saturated with mold. I was in one school where construction dust and fumes were causing whole classrooms of students to have respiratory problems.

That same school district sprayed a school with insecticide while teachers were in it (twice), causing the entire staff to require emergency room treatment.

If you have noticed that I haven't yet mentioned anything about actual teaching, it is because we really get to do very little teaching these days. We spend most of our time documenting, counseling, and disciplining before we can get to any teaching.

What are the upsides to teaching?

The good news about teaching is that if you find yourself in a bad school you are only stuck there for one year. Then you can find another school—provided you didn't do anything to antagonize the administration and cause them to give you poor recommendations.

Even with all the problems, at its best teaching can be an enormously enjoyable experience. If you are to be an effective teacher you must be constantly creative about your management of students' behavior and original in your lesson planning. As all artists know, there is nothing like setting a lot of young minds to a problem to stimulate your own creativity.

Actually, I have gotten a lot of good original ideas from my students. One thing I am interested in is designing a book of lesson plans for art teachers based on computer graphics, something that would be really useful to a teacher—not the pages of jargon usually sold to us. To be useful we must be able to learn and use it in about ten minutes—which is about all the time we have to access anything.

What advice can you offer to prospective art teachers?

I believe you should be able to do it before you can teach it. As far as being qualified to teach art, if you are an artist you can teach art. I do not believe in an art-teaching degree. I don't think any teaching degree is valid. You should have a degree in art, not art education. I think the latter should be outlawed. You must be able to do what you teach. I am able to deal with emotionally disturbed students because art school was such a horribly cruel experience for me, with constant criticism and vicious treatment from teachers and fellow students, that teaching difficult kids is no different than dealing with art professors and art students.

Temperament is another major consideration for teaching. You must have a good attitude toward people in general, with a profound respect for the individual and a knowledge of human nature.

But you should never prejudge and say (or feel) things such as "He'll never amount to much." Kids are guaranteed to make a monkey out of you every time if you prejudge them.

You must never take anything personally, either. This is especially important when dealing with problem students. If they know they can get to you they will.

Detached, concerned professionalism is best (like a doctor) to serve the students' interests. Remember, you are a powerful authority figure put in a position that can create a rebellious attitude in American youth. Don't abuse your position and don't think the kids are your friends. You will serve them best as a teacher, not a buddy; it's a special relationship and must be understood by the teacher or you will not be able to deflect the frequent abuse for which the position targets you.

Peggy Peters earned her B.F.A. from the University of Texas at San Antonio, where she majored in studio art with a painting and clay sculpture concentration. She earned her M.A. from Syracuse University in New York with a degree in illustration. She has a dual career, dividing her time between teaching and illustrating. She teaches in an alternative school in San Antonio.

INTERVIEW

Lynne Robins
Art Teacher

Tell us about your career path.

I am an artist. I visited the classroom of a gifted teacher at a Headstart program in Vermont when I was studying at Bennington College. There was no money but they were rich in ideas; brushes were made from sponges and branches, and blocks from lumber scraps and pegs. The children were happy, busy. I thought the teacher a miracle worker. I wanted to be one, too.

I switched my major from art to psychology with a concentration in art. I didn't know precisely what direction to go in. My first job offered discounted graduate-school tuition to its employees. I took advantage of this: I took the GREs, passed them, and enrolled in the grad program.

I kind of stumbled into special education, then into art as an art teacher with various programs (museum or community-based or summer schools) and finally began using art no matter where I was stationed or in what capacity, because it was a part of me and the way I functioned best.

I also stumbled into my first full-time job through a chance encounter with a social worker while I was working as an art teacher at a behavior modification summer camp. The job was at a campus lab school for handicapped children. I worked as a teacher's assistant for a regular class and as an art teacher for the entire school. I'll never forget the day some of the wheelchair kids deliberately tipped over cans of paint and wheeled through them, streaking the corridors with all manner of color tracks. It didn't hurt that they also grabbed brushes and streaked the walls as they went. I thought I would die on the spot.

I worked with deaf and multiply handicapped children and adults for nine years. The secret of my teaching was my base as an artist. I held jobs in both Massachusetts and California, working with private schools, private programs, and community colleges.

Then, I burned out and took off about four years to work as a freelancer and advertising artist. At the same time, I went back to school to receive certification in art education so that I could work as an art teacher in the public schools. My training and student teaching were exciting; my elementary classes gave me a standing ovation and my high school classes were exhilarating.

When I learned Boston was looking for teachers, I applied as a special education teacher to get into the system. My assignments were as an elementary moderate special needs teacher. However, my art training was not in vain—most of my projects with students were arts based and received recognition for both the students and myself.

How would you describe your job?

I work with special education children in grades one through five, as well as with regular education children in integrated classrooms.

I am a certified art teacher, special education teacher, and elementary teacher. I have taught in several fields, beginning with multiply handicapped deaf children and adolescents. I then switched to working with disadvantaged children in the inner-city schools.

I have a background as an artist (mixed media, metals, textbook illustration, advertising) and most of what I do as a teacher involves the same processes. Teaching is a very creative profession. It involves working with ideas and making them take root in reality. For example, a recent project with students involved studying solar energy, creating solar-powered vehicles, and painting and decorating them. The project grew into an immense undertaking that involved 8 adults and over 125 children, and which may become an after-school institute.

Making art is a problem-solving process; so is science. I believe that similarities go beyond differences conceptually. We have made artist's books, learned to write through art, created murals, used multimedia. The list is endless. Most students love to work in this manner—and the enthusiasm is often quite high.

A typical day involves working with twenty-two learning-handicapped children during six or seven block periods. Most are "pulled out" from their regular classes; sometimes I work with them in the classroom along with the entire class.

The pace is frantic; the day flies by. It's never boring, sometimes relaxing, though usually totally unpredictable. There's always something new to do or to learn with the students.

The city of Boston, as well as the country, is working with new goals and standards for education. There is a lot of curriculum change, innovation—all the elements that artists love: challenge, innovation, problems to solve, materials to utilize. I call my work creating with a human canvas.

Currently, some students are creating books by using throwaway cameras, getting prints, creating chapter heads, writing "pitchlines" of fifteen words or less for chapters, and editing them for spelling (using process-writing procedures). Then we have them bound into hardcover books. Some students may be doing independent research projects using the Internet on computers that were purchased through arts-based grants.

Others may be using multimedia arts programs (Flying Colors, Amazing Writing Machine) to create individual books, artwork, and other projects. Most of the work is monitored by goals and objectives for 766 (the special-education law) individualized for each student. Most projects take between three to six weeks.

The teaching day goes from 9 A.M. to 3:30 P.M. I often use time after school to coach students or to do an after-school class or projects in the district. There are always workshops available for teachers—lots of opportunities for professional growth and development.

My job is infinitely creative. It is challenging, process oriented, and unpredictable due to human factors—one never knows what the next minute or hour might bring.

What are the upsides and downsides of your job?

The projects, which are arts or science based, are creative in scope and thus fascinating for me to develop and to implement. I often need to get grants, write them, and have them funded. My school is multicultural—primarily black and Asian—and I enjoy the challenge and pleasures of working with people of various cultural backgrounds.

My current hangup about my work is that there is never enough time to do all we want to. The work is demanding, exhausting, and sometimes I wish there were a little less stress associated with it.

But working with children and their parents has brought me a great deal of personal happiness and joy. I can see myself working as an educator forever.

What advice would you offer to those interested in teaching?

If you want to teach, you will need to reach down deep inside yourself and ask yourself if you have the stamina, the commitment, the creativity, and the endurance.

The challenge for me has come from the fact that I happen to be deaf and am working with hearing students, which has made for many a hairy and hair-raising experience. It has been a personal journey for me, as well as a professional one—learning to deal with the nature of the beast.

Teaching has been a struggle for me, because it exposed me to the best and worst of human nature on a daily basis—my own and others'! It will call for everything you have. It will demand that you draw on resources that you didn't know existed—mental, spiritual, emotional. The payoff will come from knowing that you can make a difference in the lives of many individuals.

I found it's also important to have structure of sorts, to be able to structure even the most creative of projects, at least externally—because special ed students often work best from a structured base, going from structure to creativity.

Special education students are not necessarily the Brady Bunch—you'll need a great deal of patience and tolerance, and a sense of humor.

Lynne Robins is a special education teacher at the William Monroe Trotter School, an elementary school in Boston, Massachusetts. She studied at Bennington College in Vermont and earned her B.A. in psychology with a concentration in art. She earned her M.Ed. at Boston College in special education and most recently her M.S.A.E. (master of science in art education) from the Massachusetts College of Art.

MUSEUM STUDIES

Most people who work in art museums are, not surprisingly, art lovers. They fill a variety of functions and come to their work with a range of experience and qualifications. Not only do art lovers keep museums functioning today, they're the reason art museums started in the first place. To understand better how to nurture an art career in this setting, it's important to have an idea of the origins of the art museums.

THE HISTORY OF ART MUSEUMS

Most of the famous art museums around the world acquired their exhibitions from private art collectors, whether through voluntary donations or as the result of political changes. Historically, the principle of public control over art and art collections was firmly established in France during the Revolution: the royal collection was nationalized in 1793 and opened to the public as the Louvre.

In the late 1700s and early 1800s more and more privately owned collections became available for public view throughout the world. For example, the art collection held by King Frederick William III of Prussia led to the establishment of the Kaiser Friedrich Museum in Berlin, and the tsar's private art collection formed the exhibits at the Hermitage Museum in Saint Petersburg, Russia.

The National Collection of Fine Arts in Washington, D.C. (renamed the National Museum of American Art in 1980), was the first federal collection of American art. Established in 1846 as part of the Smithsonian Institution, in 1906 it was designated a national gallery of art.

The word *museum* comes from the ancient Greek name for the temple of the Muses, the nine beings who were the patron goddesses of the arts in Greek mythology. The term was first used to refer to institutions of advanced learning and didn't take on its current meaning until the Renaissance, when the first great collections of art were formed in Italy. During the seventeenth and eighteenth centuries art museums thrived throughout Europe. As in the Renaissance period, however, almost all collections were private, and public access was limited.

An exception was the collection of Sir Hans Sloane, which was bequeathed to Great Britain in 1753. It became the foundation for the British Museum, the first museum organized as a public institution.

In the late 1800s, several specialized museums were created in Europe, such as the Bavarian National Museum in Munich and the Museum of Ornamental Art in London, which was later renamed the Victoria and Albert Museum. The first museums to be set up as public institutions in the United States were the Museum of Fine Arts in Boston in 1870 and the Metropolitan Museum of Art in New York City in 1872. In 1879 the Art Institute of Chicago followed.

TYPES OF ART MUSEUMS

First, to understand the professional position an art lover might enjoy within an art museum, it is important to recognize the different types of art museums and the roles they play. Art museums are buildings where objects of aesthetic value are preserved and displayed. Art museums have a variety of functions, including acquiring, conserving, and exhibiting works of art; providing art education for the general public; and conducting art historical research.

Since the beginning of the twentieth century, art museums have seen a number of trends, such as the expansion of large institutions and the creation of a horde of specialized museums, many of which are devoted to modern art. In contrast, a number of the world's largest museums have attempted recently to reduce their size and improve the quality of their collections. They have begun selling less important works of art in order to concentrate available funds on acquiring works of greater artistic merit or historical significance.

Art museums can be classified into two major categories: private museums, under the authority of a board of trustees composed of private citizens and a director chosen by the board, and public museums, administered directly by the national or local government.

In addition, art museums fall into two basic types: the general museum, presenting a broad range of works from early times to the present, and museums that specialize in one particular era, artist, region, or type of art.

In recent years, costs for building maintenance, staff, utilities, and insurance have escalated—while federal funding has decreased. How art museums support themselves has become a controversial issue. Once free to the public, many museums now charge admission. Membership subscriptions are aggressively sought as another major source of revenue. Most public museums now also solicit donations from individuals and businesses, and vie for corporate and government grants. These practices, while both legal and ethical, affect a museum's choices by forcing it to give precedence to those exhibitions and acquisitions that can be funded by outside sources.

In other words, the art you see displayed in a museum might not have been chosen for its aesthetic value alone, but for its ability to, at least in part, raise income. Exhibitions with mass appeal are most likely to find financial sponsorship; art that is less familiar to the general public is less likely to be funded.

This cold reality often creates a dilemma for a museum's director and acquisitions curator, but most museum professionals stand by their objectivity, frequently having to defend their independent position in spite of the preferences of patrons.

Natural history museums, dedicated to research, exhibition, and education in the natural sciences, are also included in this career track. In addition to the expected collections of gems and jewels, fossils, meteorites, and animals from around the world displayed in lifelike settings, natural history museums also handle collections that include artifacts from ancient civilizations. The responsibility for restoring and maintaining these artifacts falls to the conservators, discussed later in this chapter.

Living history museums provide artists and artisans with interesting employment. (Read about this popular work setting in Chapter 3.)

JOB TITLES WITHIN ART MUSEUMS

In the past, art museums functioned mainly as storehouses for objects, but in recent years their role has been greatly expanded. More and more large art museums try to serve the interests of the community in which they are located. In addition to exhibiting their own collections, many museums develop special "traveling" exhibitions that are loaned out to other institutions for display. They also conduct guided tours of their collections, publish catalogs and books, provide lectures and other educational programs to members of the general public, and offer art classes to students. With all these varied roles, art museums can now offer a wealth of employment opportunities to job seekers.

Art Museum Curators   Curators in art museums are responsible for the preservation of the collection and for implementing its visual accessibility to the public. The curator is usually an art historian knowledgeable about the physical properties of handmade objects. While curators have a general background in the history of art, they usually specialize in a given area. Large museums with diversified collections employ several curators for the different departments, such as American, European, modern, Oriental, and primitive art; decorative arts; and photography.

Curators oversee the collection and participate in obtaining new acquisitions. They also verify the authenticity of a painting or object by researching its provenance, a document attesting to the work's previous owners and exhibitors.

The curator also supervises the installation of the museum's permanent collection. He or she determines the number of objects to be shown and decides when to show them. Working with the exhibit designer, the curator also plans how objects or paintings will be displayed.

Associate curators and/or curatorial assistants report directly to the curator and help with the varied tasks the profession demands.

Art and Object Conservators

Many people think that once something valuable gets into a museum, it's safe. Unfortunately, art decays on the museum's walls or shelves just as fast as it would decay on yours at home. Many different conditions contribute to that decaying process: light, variations in humidity and temperature, pollutants, pests, and accidental damage. Conservators concern themselves with preventing that decay.

Art conservators, once known as art or painting restorers, preserve and restore damaged and faded paintings. They apply solvents and cleaning agents to clean the surfaces, reconstruct or retouch damaged areas, and apply preservatives to protect the paintings.

Object conservators help prevent deterioration through a number of steps:

1. *Examination* of the object to determine its nature, properties, method of manufacture, and the causes of deterioration

2. *Scientific analysis and research* on the object to identify methods and materials

3. *Documentation* of the condition of the object before, during, and after treatment, and to record actual treatment methods

4. *Preventive measures* to minimize further damage by providing a controlled environment

5. *Treatment* to stabilize objects or slow their deterioration

6. *Restoration*, when necessary, to bring an object closer to its original appearance

Registrars

Registrars in art museums keep track of the location of all the various works of art in the museum's collection. Paintings and other art objects are often moved to different areas within a museum, or they are transported to other museums for exhibition. Thus, it is essential to maintain accurate records and files. Registrars are also responsible for shipping objects and obtaining insurance.

Collections Managers

The collections manager supervises, numbers, catalogs, and stores the specimens within each division of the museum. An undergraduate degree in the area of the museum's specialization is the minimum requirement for this position. An advanced degree in museum studies with a concentration in a specific discipline is recommended.

A collections manager must be proficient in information management techniques and be able to accurately identify objects within the museum's collection. Knowledge of security practices and environmental controls is also important.

Art Historians

Art historians research and write about works of art. They may also deliver lectures on art history and advise others about art. An art historian has to be knowledgeable about the history of art, past and present theories of art, past and present ways of making art, research methods, different cultures, and sources of art history information, including libraries and art galleries.

Art historians can be employed full-time by an art museum or work independently as a consultant. Art historians also work in universities as lecturers, professors, or researchers; in art galleries as curators or consultants; in auction houses as buyers or consultants; and at historic sites, buildings, and monuments as consultants. Within art museums, art historians often work in the role of art curator.

Photographers

Many art museums keep a professional photographer on staff to provide photographic documentation of the various fine arts collections. The photographer also oversees the photography of general museum events and activities. He or she is responsible for studio and darkroom facilities and personnel issues concerning assistants.

Many photographers are self-taught; others receive their training in a variety of ways: through traditional art schools, through university art and photography departments, and through apprenticeships.

A portfolio documenting professional experience is a requirement for employment as an art museum photographer. Photographers also find work in planetariums and other types of museums.

Educators

Almost all museums provide some sort of educational programming for the public, which is designed and arranged by museum educators and program developers. They explain the exhibits and conduct classes, workshops, lectures, and tours. They often offer outreach programs to the schools or the local community in which the museum is located. Educators usually possess a teaching certificate or have had teaching experience before they join a museum staff.

Tour Guides/Docents

Although most museums rely on volunteer help to act as tour guides and docents (the two job titles have essentially the same meaning), there are still a few spots for a paid professional. Most tour guides have a college degree in either education or the field of study the particular museum encompasses.

TRAINING AND QUALIFICATIONS

With museums offering so many diverse careers, it stands to reason that avenues of training leading to these professions would be equally diverse. An art conservator would have a background different from that of a taxidermist; an educator's preparation would differ from an exhibit designer's.

In addition, different museums often look for different qualifications. Some prefer candidates to have an advanced degree or certificate in museology or museum studies. Others expect to hire professionals with strong academic concentrations in, for example, art history, history, or anthropology. Most are impressed with a combination of academic and hands-on training earned through internships or volunteer programs.

Several skills and personal traits, however, are common to all museum professionals. For a start, all museum workers need to have excellent interpersonal skills. Educators, tour guides, and exhibit designers present information to staff and visitors; directors and curators supervise staff and cultivate contacts with donors and other community members; interpreters, security guards, and museum gift shop staff constantly interact with visitors; museum support staff must interact with one another, and so on. The ability to get along with others and to work well with others as a team is a vital asset in museum work.

Of equal importance is the ability to communicate through the written word. Museums meet their missions with their collections of objects, but to do so, museum workers must have strong writing skills. Good written language skills show themselves in grant applications, exhibition catalogs, brochures, administrative and scholarly reports, training and educational materials, legal agreements, interpretive labeling for exhibits, object records, and much more.

Other personal characteristics and abilities are also crucial. Before pursuing formal training leading to a career in museum work, review the following list. How many of these characteristics apply to you?

- Strong people skills

- Excellent speaking and writing skills

- Manual dexterity

- A good imagination

- Creativity

- A healthy curiosity

- Resourcefulness

- Commitment to education

- Patience

- Flexibility

- Problem-solving ability

- Ability to handle multiple tasks

- An understanding of the mission of museums and how they go about achieving it

- Business skills

- Computer skills

While many items on this checklist are natural skills, many can also be learned. The last item, computer skills, deserves additional mention. More and more museums are relying on computers to keep track of their collections, to design labels, and to produce catalogs and brochures, as well as other functions. Ease in working with a variety of software programs can be only an asset to a prospective museum worker.

How you proceed will depend upon your interests and circumstances. If you are clear from the start what avenue you wish to pursue, you can customize a course of study for yourself at the university of your choosing. Courses you'll take or the degree toward which you'll work will depend in part on whether you are a new student or are returning to school to supplement your education for the museum profession.

Traditionally, new hires to the field of museum work have completed bachelor's and master's degrees in academic disciplines appropriate to the intended career. Curators for art museums have studied art and art history; curators for natural history museums have studied biology, anthropology, archaeology, and so on. And while such a background still serves as the main foundation for successful museum work, for the last thirty years or so more and more people have explored university programs offering practical and theoretical training in the area of museum studies. Courses such as museum management, curatorship, fundraising, exhibition development, and museum law offer a more specific approach to the work at hand. This, coupled with a broad background in liberal arts or specialization in an academic discipline, provides the museum professional with a knowledge base better designed to serve the needs of the museum.

Whatever your course of study, these days most museums require a graduate degree, either in an academic discipline or in museum studies, museum science, or museology. Also required is an intensive internship or record of long-term volunteer work.

What follows is a list of three possible tracks with which a student can proceed to prepare for a career in museums:

Track One

Bachelor's degree in general museum studies, museology, or museum science

Master's degree or doctorate in a specific academic discipline

Internship arranged through the university or directly with a museum in a particular field

Track Two

Bachelor's degree in liberal arts or a specific academic discipline

Master's degree or certificate in museum studies, museology, or museum science

Internship arranged through the university or directly with a museum in a particular field

Track Three (for the museum professional upgrading skills)

Master's degree or certificate in museum studies; *or*

Noncredit-bearing certificate in museum studies (short-term course)

The internship is considered the most crucial practical learning experience and is generally a requirement in all museum programs. Internships can last from ten weeks to a year with varying time commitments per week.

Curator Training

Employment as a curator generally requires graduate education and substantial practical or work experience. Many curators work in museums while completing their formal education, in order to gain the hands-on experience that many employers seek when hiring.

In most museums, a master's degree in an appropriate discipline of the museum's specialty—for example, art, history, or archaeology or museum studies—is required for employment as a curator. Many employers prefer a doctoral degree, particularly for curators in natural history or science museums. In small museums, curatorial positions may be available to individuals with a bachelor's degree. For some positions, an internship of full-time museum work supplemented by courses in museum studies is needed.

Museum Technician Training

Museum technicians generally need a bachelor's degree in an appropriate discipline of the museum's specialty, museum studies training, or previous museum work experience, particularly in exhibit design.

Technician positions often serve as a stepping-stone for individuals interested in curatorial work. With the exception of small museums, a master's degree is needed for advancement.

Art Historian Training

At least a B.A. with a major in art history is required to enter the profession, but most employers prefer a postgraduate degree in art history.

Conservator Training

Conservators are a group of highly trained professionals who have gone through a number of steps to gain their expertise. Training programs are few and, as a result, are very competitive.

According to the American Institute for Conservation of Historic and Artistic Works, a conservator must have the following qualities:

- Appreciation and respect for cultural property of all kinds—their historic and sociological significance, their aesthetic qualities, and the technology of their production

- Aptitude for scientific and technical subjects

- Patience for meticulous and tedious work

- Good manual dexterity and color vision

- Intelligence and sensitivity for making sound judgments

- Ability to communicate effectively

During the course of a training program, student conservators are exposed to work with a variety of materials before going on to specialize in a particular area. They learn skills to prevent the deterioration of paintings, paper and books, fiber, textiles, ceramics, wood, furniture, and other objects. Some conservators even specialize in architectural conservation and library and archives conservation.

Training most traditionally is gained through a graduate academic program, which takes from two to four years. Apprenticeships or internships are a vital part of training and are usually conducted during the final year of study. Some programs might offer internships that run concurrently with classes.

Admission requirements for the various graduate programs differ, but all the programs require academic prerequisites, including courses in chemistry, art history, studio art, anthropology, and archaeology.

Some programs prefer candidates who already have a strong background in conservation, which can be gained through undergraduate apprenticeships and fieldwork in private, regional, or institutional conservation laboratories.

A personal interview is also usually a requirement of the application process. A candidate's portfolio must demonstrate manual dexterity as well as familiarity with materials and techniques.

Careful planning at the undergraduate level will help improve your chances of acceptance into a graduate program, but because acceptance is very competitive, it is not unusual to have to repeat the application process. Before reapplying, however, it is a good idea to enhance your standing by undertaking additional studies or fieldwork. Many programs, on request, will review your resume and suggest avenues for further study.

THE JOB HUNT

Although formal, academic training is vital to a resume, hands-on experience is of equal importance. Not only does it provide a host of significant skills, it also allows the career explorer to make an informed decision about the suitability of museum work. A person who starts with a term of volunteer work, even before beginning a college program, will have a better idea of what career options museums have to offer and whether these options are right for him or her.

Many museums rely heavily on volunteer energy and can place volunteers in almost every museum department, from tour guide and gift shop sales to assisting curators and exhibit designers. The easiest way to volunteer your time is to call a museum and ask to speak to the volunteer coordinator. He or she will work with you to match your interests with the museum's needs. Volunteer programs are usually flexible about the number of hours and days per week they expect from their volunteers.

Most academic museum studies programs require an internship before a degree or certificate can be awarded. In addition, many museums have their own internship programs that are offered to full-time students as well as recent graduates. You can check with your university department first to see what arrangements they traditionally make. If the burden is on you to arrange an internship, either during your academic program or after you've graduated, contact the museum's internship coordinator. If the museum has no formal internship program, talk first to a museum staff member to determine where there might be a need. Then write a proposal incorporating your interests in a department where help will be appreciated.

Internships can be either paid or unpaid and are usually a more formal arrangement than volunteering. The number of hours and weeks is structured, and many interns are expected to complete specific projects during their time at the museum. Often, college credit is awarded for internships.

The following four reports published by the American Association of Museums are helpful sources of information about different museum professions and how to conduct a successful job search in this field. They may be ordered by writing to the following address:

American Association of Museums
Attn.: Bookstore
P.O. Box 4002
Washington, DC 20042-4002

1. *Careers in Museums: A Variety of Vocations*: This publication gives a broad overview of professional career opportunities in museums, suggests educational qualifications and experience for specific positions, and provides information on how to obtain internships. It also lists job placement resources.

2. *Museum Studies Programs: Guide to Evaluation*: Refer to this guide for answers to questions about the curriculum and quality of museum studies programs.

3. *Guide to Museum Studies and Training in the United States*: This publication provides information on training opportunities, internships and fellowships, mid-career opportunities, and management programs.

4. *Standards and Guidelines for Museum Internships*: This pamphlet clarifies what museums expect from their interns and what interns can and should expect from the museums.

EARNINGS

Earnings of curators vary considerably by type and size of employer, and often by specialty. Average salaries in the federal government, for example, are generally higher than those in religious organizations. Salaries of curators in large, well-funded museums may be several times higher than those in small ones.

The average annual salary for all museum curators in the federal government in nonsupervisory, supervisory, and managerial positions was about $55,000 in 1997.

According to a survey by the Association of Art Museum Directors, median salaries for selected workers in larger art museums are as follows:

Director	$103,000
Curator	50,000
Art historian	50,000
Senior conservator	48,500
Museum technician	36,300
Curatorial assistant	22,600

INTERVIEW

Erica Hirshler
Assistant Curator, Museum of Fine Arts, Boston

What is a typical day like for you at the museum?

There is no typical day; it's a very seat-of-the-pants type of schedule. My duties range a great deal. We have 2,000 paintings in the collection and not every one has been studied for its historical significance. I study and work on the permanent collection, organize special exhibitions, do research, write catalogs and art books, write label copy and brochure copy for exhibitions, and arrange for the display of different things in the galleries.

I also handle a lot of correspondence with the general public; we get a lot of inquiries. They range from people who have a painting in their attic and don't know what it is to scholars who are working on projects at other institutions and need information on our collection. And I administer the loan requests for our department.

Our paintings department has a European side and an American side, and on the American side, where I work, there is a curator, an associate curator, and myself, assistant curator, and four research assistants and fellows of varying areas of specialization.

I like working with the objects—it's a special thrill working with the real thing that you don't get from slides. I'm interested in them as physical objects. You gather them together for a special exhibition; you get to really examine them.

But there's never enough time to do everything you'd like to do. There's a lot of paperwork. It would be nice if there were less paperwork and more time to work on scholarly things. Research is important.

You could be doing lots of different things for $30,000 a year. I really love what I do or I wouldn't be doing it.

What advice would you offer someone interested in a career as a museum curator?

Of course, it's every assistant curator's hope to move up the curatorial ladder. There's usually more money and prestige involved with a promotion. Often, to move ahead, a curator would have to be willing to change locations. But opportunities can be limited. Sometimes it's better to stay right where you are.

We have one of the two best collections of American paintings in the country—the Metropolitan Museum of Art in New York City has the other—so you balance the strength of being in an institution that values your field against some of the other things that might not be so positive—in other words, moving to a weaker collection to get a better title. It wouldn't be worth it.

Going to a smaller museum with a smaller collection isn't necessarily a good career move unless you're interested in getting onto a director track. You could be a director at a small museum, then eventually a director at a bigger museum. But the more administrative your job becomes the less work you can do as a scholar.

People who do well in this career are very flexible about how their work time is structured. It's not a job where you can disappear for a year and write your book. You have to be willing to roll with the punches and be able to juggle several projects simultaneously.

You'll have a couple of different exhibitions you're working on at the same time. One might be coming along in two years; one might be in two months. And you go back and forth between them. Or you'll have three different catalog deadlines for three different shows. You have to write your manuscript and turn it in to the editor.

Erica Hirshler began work at the Museum of Fine Arts as a volunteer in 1983. Only four months later she was offered a paying, part-time job, which two years later developed into a full-time position as assistant curator. Erica earned her B.A. from Wellesley in art history and medieval studies in 1979, and her M.A. in art history and a museum studies diploma from Boston University in 1983. In January 1992 she earned her Ph.D. in art history, also from Boston University. The Museum of Fine Arts in Boston has been in existence for more than 125 years. The museum covers collections from all over the world with more than one million objects.

INTERVIEW

Aileen Chuk
Associate Registrar, Metropolitan Museum of Art

Tell us about your job.

As administrative manager, I work directly with the head registrar taking care of all personnel issues and supervising the work of junior staff members.

While a small museum might have only one registrar, a large museum such as the Metropolitan Museum of Art in New York City needs a much bigger staff to cover all the responsibilities of an expansive and active collection.

Currently, in addition to the head registrar, the Metropolitan has four people handling exhibits, two working with outgoing museum loans, one dealing with loans to the museum and exams (items brought in for review), a storeroom manager, one conservator and one assistant to the conservator (in addition to the many conservators working in the conservation department), and four packers.

The rankings for registrars at the Metropolitan Museum of Art are as follows: assistant registrar, senior assistant registrar, associate registrar, and head registrar.

A registrar has a lot of functions, depending on the size of the institution. At the Metropolitan we have certain duties, mostly involving shipping of artworks. We take care of the packing, we make the transportation arrangements, arrange for couriers, take care of the insurance, and keep an archive of all of the works that are lent to the museum.

In smaller museums the registrars will sometimes do condition checking of objects and other exhibition duties, but at the Metropolitan we have a very defined purpose and there are a lot of stratas of responsibility. For instance, each curatorial department in the museum—and there are eighteen of them—keeps its own storage rooms. They control their inventories, but we perform inventory spot checks within those departments on a yearly basis to make sure their records are in place.

Basically, a curator decides what he or she is going to have in a particular show and gives you a list of some two hundred objects. Then it's your problem. You have to make sure the loan agreements are signed and in place, make all the packing arrangements, contact the borrowers or the lenders to the museum, coordinate scheduling of shipments and courier arrangements, then make arrangements for the unpacking of those objects here. You coordinate with the conservation staff to check those works in concert with the curatorial staff.

I love my work. It's varied and interesting. For instance, you may be dealing with very small Impressionist paintings on one exhibition, then you may be dealing with massive, several-thousand-pound twentieth-century sculptures for the next exhibition. Each show you do provides you with a whole new set of challenges.

I had to deal with collecting a work from a person's house in Omaha, and it was very difficult to even get the work out of the house. It was an oversized, contemporary painting that had originally been rolled to get inside. To get it out, it had to be taken off its stretcher, brought outside to an open area, put back on the stretcher, then packed into a crate, then put on a truck. But the crate was something like 20 feet high by 100 feet long, and I had to coordinate all this from New York.

I had to find the right people to do the job, people who would be very familiar with artwork and up to the standards you expect. You don't want them to damage it. Then I had to coordinate all arrangements with the lender, and make sure it was done carefully and properly and on time.

I contacted the local museums out there and was referred to someone who had done this kind of work before. He was able to go to the person's house and send me specifications of what he suggested needed to be done. Sometimes it takes years of experience to be able to coordinate something like this.

What are the upsides and downsides of your job?

It takes a lot of personal time and frequently takes away from your family life. There's a lot of overtime.

Shipments come at two o'clock in the morning or they leave at five in the morning. Then there's a lot of traveling involved, escorting artworks, and sometimes you want to do it, and then it's a real plus to the job, but sometimes you don't. You might have just come back from vacation, or you'll be missing your daughter's piano recital, or you have a lot of work piling up that you need to get to.

But I've been almost everywhere: Germany, France, Italy, Switzerland five times, Japan twice a couple of years ago. It can be very rewarding and lots of fun, but sometimes the demands are such that you're trying to do an enormous amount of work in your office and prepare for a courier trip at the same time.

Salaries can be another downside. Museum work can be extremely rewarding, but it's not a career suited for someone who is interested in making a lot of money.

But all the negative issues aside, it's still very rewarding. You get to see a project from its inception to its completion. You have the knowledge that you've been part of a very large effort to put on a show of major proportions.

You work very much as part of a team. One of the nice things about working at the Metropolitan in the registrar's office is that the curatorial departments are really separate entities: they all have their own specialties; they tend to focus within the area of history they work with. Someone in European paintings may not have a lot to do with the Asian art department, for example. But in the registrar's office we are dealing with all eighteen departments, so you're involved with eighteen different types of art, as well as a huge variety of people with different specialties. You're the central core for all the flow and traffic in and out of the building.

What advice would you give to others considering this field?

You need a definite mentality. You need to be very detail oriented and very organized.

You're usually juggling two hundred artworks and you have to remember all the details for all those artworks and what the lenders are requiring. You have to really be able to have a good memory; it's essential. You document things in a lot of different ways, but you also have to keep them in your head at the same time.

And though I've seen people who've done this without an art background, I think it would be very helpful to have one. Generally, throughout the field, registrars tend to have an interest in art. Either they're artists themselves or they have painting skills or some artistic bent. Most have a bachelor's degree in art history. If you're really serious, you should pursue a preliminary degree in art so you have a familiarity with it. We deal with a lot of diverse materials and it helps to have an understanding of the physical properties of artwork.

A lot of the work is learned on the job. And there are museum studies programs that grant certificates. You learn the administration of the museum. Many people go that route after receiving their bachelor's degree. It's a good way to get your foot in the door. We get a lot of interns from those programs—an internship is the best way to find out how a museum functions, and that's very important.

There are a number of different specialties within the registrar's office. And the more senior you get, the more complex work you're assigned. As you gain experience you tend to do exhibitions rather than museum loans or other various tasks that might be in the department. It usually starts at something quite low. If you started with exhibitions, you'd usually start with very small shows. Normally people work their way up the ranks, starting with exams, then work to loans, then go to exhibitions.

Aileen Chuk worked for eleven years at the Museum of Modern Art in New York before coming to the Metropolitan in 1994. She has a bachelor's degree in art history from Fordham University in New York and serves a dual role at the museum as administrative manager and associate registrar.

INTERVIEW

Joan Gardner
Chief Conservator, Carnegie Museum of Natural History

How did you get started in this field?

I had been a science and math teacher and a social worker, then decided to change careers and went back to school as an adult. I was involved in a joint program with George Washington University and the Smithsonian Institution.

My thesis director took me to the Smithsonian, where they had just developed a program in museum studies with a conservation component. When I walked into the lab I knew then that that was what I wanted to do. I'd always been fascinated with anthropology and archaeology in particular. You can't get into this profession without being fascinated with the objects that people produce in various cultures around the world, and what these objects mean, and why they're done the way they are. They're often so beautiful, but you just don't know, until you get into anthropology, what it all means. Sometimes you don't even know then.

I was enrolled in a special studies program for my master's degree (the program is no longer offered) with an emphasis in conservation. It was split between anthropology and art history, and I had a strong science background. There's an emphasis on a lot of chemistry.

All programs have an internship. I did mine at the Smithsonian during the entire three years. It was almost a full-time job for me, fitting classes in between my hours at the Smithsonian. I got my master's degree in 1976, then came directly to Carnegie.

Tell us about your work at the museum.

The Carnegie collections are worldwide in distribution, focusing on traditional natural history areas including botany, zoology, geology, paleontology, minerals, gems, and anthropology. An objects conservator for a natural history museum probably sees a wider range of items than your average art museum conservator. I work with a comfortable variety of anthropological objects, including skins, hides, fur, Indian robes, wooden dolls, and feathered headdresses. Many of these garments and items were not meant to last longer than a few years, but some of them have now lasted several hundred. A conservator's efforts show long-lasting results.

We don't do a lot of restoration work. We try to keep the object's integrity intact as much as possible. Restoration is often conceived of as trying to bring something back to its condition when it was new. That's not what we're after at all. We want to slow down further deterioration, but we're not necessarily someone who wants to put it back. We wouldn't take a sword that's ancient and make it shiny and look as if it were fabricated the day before yesterday. That's not our purpose. We want something to look cared for; we do care for the objects, and if they need treatment we will do it.

But we'll document it and try to use only materials that are compatible and we know have proven to be reversible or will not interfere and cause some sort of contamination to the object. We try not to use any replacement pieces. If we have to, we try to use something compatible with the piece. We don't just arbitrarily use a new feather, for example, because it probably wouldn't be the right feather.

As an example, one of the things I've worked with is a Hopi headdress that a child would wear. It's made of wood and painted, with feathers and leather straps. Then we have these huge headdresses from the Plains groups such as the Crow, the Arapaho, and the Lakota (formerly known as Sioux). They're made with dyed horsehair and eagle feathers and go from the top of the warrior's head and trail to the ground.

I also deal with Kachina dolls, which come from the Southwest. Most were produced by Hopi tribes, as well as others. They represent different spirits, usually made of wood, and have an earthly component and spiritual component. The Hopi used them to get their gods to bring rain or fortuitous events, and as a training tool for children in the Hopi household.

They have all kinds of accoutrements such as bows and arrows and feathered headdresses. They're almost always painted and sometimes have outfits on that are very complicated.

I'm also working on a bentwood box from the Northwest Coast Indian group named Haida. I do research into the materials it was made from, how it was made, the colorants, the red, the black, the blue, the green, what they are. We can take samples and send them off for analysis or you might use your own microscope to try to determine the origin of the dye or paint.

The bentwood box is badly abraded and broken in many places and someone had previously hammered in steel nails all over it. Well, that's not compatible with what it looked like in the beginning. So, I won't touch it until I document what it looks like now, where the breaks are, where the new and modern materials have been used on it. Just to say it's a bentwood box doesn't tell you that much. We talk about the colors, the design, the technique that was used to cut out the design, the technique that was used to make it a bentwood box.

We document its condition; we state, "there's a fracture that's five millimeters long at the right corner." We take photographs of it before we work on it, during the time we work on it, and then after we're finished. What we're really trying to do is document what an object is made of, what we used on it, and why we did it, so there's a record for history. We're record keepers as well as people who intervene.

After documenting its original condition, I will most likely remove those modern materials and use adhesives that are reversible, so in seventy-five years you can apply a little ethanol and get that adhesive out and put a different one in if something better comes on the market.

I don't just shine it up and, if the red looks a little faded in a spot, I don't just put on some modern red. I will clean off soot and particulates, if I can without doing damage to the paint. But I'm not here to take a modern red and brighten it up.

That doesn't mean that I wouldn't try to obscure some of the terrible abrasion points that when you look at it you think, "Oh, isn't that in pitiful shape." You would tone those down, but you would completely document what you've done so nobody misunderstands where you've been and what the original object was. You don't want to obscure the original artist's work at all.

Here we have a real problem with particulates and soot. Pittsburgh has been an industrial city for a hundred years. That comes right through and settles on the objects unless they're enclosed. In the early days most objects were displayed on open shelves. They didn't have the great storage cabinetry we have now. One of our biggest jobs is to try to remove the soot. It turns the objects practically gray and you can't see the vibrant blues and reds. To remove that without damaging the pigment or diluting it is quite a feat.

What are the positive and negative aspects of your job?

For me, working with the objects is the best part of my job, dealing with the colors and the textures and the research to see what's happened to it in the past.

It's such a constant challenge, and as much as I love it, sometimes I get weary. It's a big job, overwhelming, and sometimes you can't really put it to bed at night. I do a lot of reading in the evenings to find out, for example, what the latest feather-cleaning technique is. I go through a lot of journals to find an article that's pertinent. That for me is the only downside. I love what I do.

What advice would you offer to prospective conservators?

By the time you graduate with your master's degree, you will be a skilled conservator. But unfortunately, walking into a job is not a shoo-in. Not every museum has a conservator.

Very often a museum will send their work to a private conservator because they can't afford to have a full-time conservator on staff. We do occasionally hire a private conservator to work with us. Now we have two private conservators working with us on the new hall we're setting up. I couldn't possibly get all these objects ready by myself. I only have one assistant and I need help for this project.

Some museums have two or three conservators for fine arts and/or objects. But a lot of the smaller ones don't have anybody. There are jobs out there but not nearly as many that there once were. A lot of new graduates go into private practice. Although it is expensive for a new graduate to set up a private practice (the lab chemicals alone are very costly), once in practice, an independent conservator can do quite well.

It's expensive to train people in conservation and only a few graduate each year. Before you go for your master's, you have to demonstrate a good knowledge of chemistry, you have to be good with your hands, and you have to be really bright. Almost every student has some talent, in painting, pottery, working with metals. Most people have a portfolio before they go on for their master's degree.

Your graduate program should cover theory as well as practical experience. After receiving your master's degree, you can specialize. Usually by the time you're a third-year student you know what you want to specialize in. If, for example, you know you want to go into textiles, you find a museum and intern in that area. For instance, the assistant conservator here went through the Buffalo program and he spent two years working on all kinds of objects, doing theory, dealing with the different kinds of materials, and analysis, and special research projects. But he found that he really wanted to work with Native American material. So he did an internship at Arizona State Museum, a museum that specializes in anthropological objects, mostly ethnographic and archaeology, so he was in just the right spot. Now he's here working with us as we get ready for our new Native American Hall.

It's a wonderful profession but you have to have an awful lot of skill. I don't want to minimize that. Not only must you master the information, but you have to be able to deal with things that require an awful lot of patience. My master's work comprised unfolding and stabilizing some fabrics that were in a mound, buried in 1200 A.D. They were so dry, you would touch them and they'd shatter in your hands. Frankly, it's not something that most people have the patience for.

Joan Gardner is chief conservator at the Carnegie Museum of Natural History in Pittsburgh, Pennsylvania. It is the fifth-largest natural history museum in the United States with a collection of more than seventeen million specimens and artifacts. It is also one of the nation's largest private research museums that is not associated with a university.

ART SALES

Art museums display works of art for the appreciation of all. But many art lovers are not content with only the occasional visit to a museum. They want to view art on a full-time basis and own pieces of art they can enjoy in their homes or offices.

Artists do not create in a vacuum. While many do prefer to produce art for art's sake alone, many others are happy to make their work available to the public and want and need to make a living from their work. The artist, though skilled in his or her own particular area, might not be comfortable in the world of art sales. The business side of art isn't always something that comes naturally. But that's where art galleries and art gallery professionals come in.

Art galleries are generally privately owned and are similar to specialized museums in which the collection is restricted to the works of a single artist. Art galleries can also focus on a specific historical period, category of art, or geographical region.

Art galleries operate differently from art museums. While the museum depends on membership and grants to support itself, an art gallery must earn its keep by selling works of art to the public.

Who owns art galleries? Art lovers, of course. You can't open and operate a gallery without having a strong love as well as a deep understanding for the world of art.

Who works in art galleries? More art lovers. But the list doesn't end there. Included also are art aficionados with a flair for selling and studio artists earning extra money to make ends meet—in a setting where they will be in constant contact with other artists and art lovers.

JOBS IN ART GALLERIES

Some art galleries are small with only one or two employees in addition to the director/owner. Large galleries, especially those in New York, maintain a staff of ten, fifteen, or twenty people, most of whom carry the title of assistant director.

Typical jobs found in art galleries are described in the following paragraphs.

Director/Owner

The owner of an art gallery is responsible for every aspect of running the gallery, from selecting which artists to exhibit to designing the layout of the show, hanging the artwork, promoting the show and the gallery, and selling to clients.

Art Curator/Assistant Director

A large gallery could have ten or so art curators or assistant directors. These individuals work directly with the owner, representing the gallery and reflecting the owner's taste. They also work with customers (or clients, as they are frequently called), discussing the artwork and making sales.

Rather than hiring a full-time curator, some smaller art galleries might contract work out to a curator on a show-to-show basis. (See the interview with Elizabeth English later in this chapter.)

Packager/Maintenance Personnel

Most large galleries have "backroom staff," personnel responsible for packaging purchased pieces of art for shipping and who, under the direction of the director or an assistant director or curator, hang the paintings in designated positions.

In many cases packagers or maintenance personnel are artists who take a menial job in a gallery to allow them to continue to paint and be involved in some level in the art world. If you're interested in becoming an assistant director it's also a good way to get your foot in the door. It puts you in contact with the art arena while offering you an opportunity to learn. You'll hear why they're showing particular artists, how they're exhibiting them, and what is being done to publicize the shows. It's always worthwhile to know every aspect of the business, and these so-called menial jobs are very important.

Framer

Most small galleries farm out their work to frame shops, but the larger galleries often have a framer on staff who is skilled in cutting mats for prints and cutting frames for canvases. However, most artists deliver their work to galleries already framed, so the need for professional framers hired directly by a gallery is small. But framemakers often freelance their work to a variety of galleries or organizations, have their own shops, and sometimes design and build their own line of frames. (See the interview with framemaker Rodney Stephens later in this chapter.)

Receptionist

Many large galleries, especially those in New York, hire receptionists to greet customers and answer questions over the phone. They must be knowledgeable about the artwork shown and be able to intelligently discuss different aspects of the work. Most receptionists have a degree in art; many use the position as a stepping-stone to assistant director.

THE TRAINING YOU'LL NEED

To prepare for a job in an art gallery, a degree in art would be beneficial, whether in art history or applied arts. But it can be done without it. Job candidates are also evaluated on their presence and how articulate and extroverted—without being pushy—they are.

Sales skills can be learned on the job, but a candidate must bring to the job a sincerity about art and an ability to talk about art on any level—historic or modern day.

EARNINGS

Most galleries work on a 50-50 percentage basis with the artist. But if it's a very popular artist, the gallery might take only 30 percent. The cost of the artwork could range from $2,000 for a small wooden mask to $10,000 or $50,000 or more for paintings.

Assistant directors can work on a straight salary arrangement or, as is most likely, salary plus commissions on the work sold—or even solely on a commission basis.

INTERVIEW

Matthew Carone
Gallery Owner

Tell us about your business and how you got started.

I am the owner and my wife is my partner. My son had been an assistant director, but he recently left to work for our symphony here. Now I'm semiretired. I spend five months of the year in Lenox, Massachusetts, in the Tanglewood area where I have a studio and the rest of the time in Florida with the gallery.

South Florida's busy season is during the winter months. I've found over the years that during the summer months, if you're lucky, you just make ends meet, so we decided many years ago not to worry about the summers, to just relax, and when people are back in the momentum of buying we open our doors and everyone is clamoring to come in and see what's new for the year.

I now have a track record so I am in a position where I can be very selective. There are a number of artists who would like to show with me. After you have

established yourself you get to that plateau where the artist knows of your reputation and wants to be in your stable of artists, so to speak.

But when you're starting, you have to trust your taste and look for talent that
is yet to be discovered. Establish yourself as a serious gallery. I happened to do
it by way of master graphics. I got involved with original prints, not reproductions, but very serious Picassos, very serious Cézanne and Matisse prints, and I
got a reputation for that in the early years. This made it easier for me to then
work one-on-one with important artists because they knew of my seriousness.

Many of the sources for these prints happened to be in Europe, which allowed
me to go there every two or three months. The most important dealers in Europe
met once a month to discuss what was happening in the art world, what was new,
what was fake, that sort of thing. As it turned out, I had discovered a Picasso fake
and got a lot of mileage and publicity through that.

I'm color-blind, but I became value sensitive. I can see the value of a color,
the lightness or darkness, more so than a person with normal color vision. The
ink used for this one Picasso was called an ivory black, which is the blackest of
blacks, but I knew that the originals had a warmer black. On the basis of that I
knew there was something wrong, so I went to Paris and showed it to a very important Picasso dealer. He said to me, "Mr. Carone, if you had showed me this print
framed, under glass, I would have said it was OK, but you're right, this is a fake."
This led me to Picasso's biggest dealer, but my biggest mistake was when he said
he must show this to Picasso—I should have insisted that I go along with that
print, but I didn't do that.

They sent it to him and Picasso did send it back to me. He had written "Faux,"
or fake, on the print and had drawn a line through it. But Picasso also signed it,
meaning "Picasso says faux," so it then achieved some value. Anything he put
his name to had value, and the faux print became an interesting thing to see. A
prominent international auction house said that the print was very good, so who-
ever the artist was, he had a lot of talent. The fake was terrific. The FBI, of course,
got involved with this; they had an idea who he was, but it was never pursued
because it's very difficult to prove. They never found out.

This event came at that time of my life when I was getting involved seriously
and it gave me a new level of importance. Everybody started banging on my door
wanting me to look at their Picassos. Now, over the years I've developed a clientele that comes to me for particulars.

How do you successfully sell art?

I always felt that you never sell a painting—you sell yourself first. That's really
a barometer for selling. And if I really love something, it's the easiest thing in
the world for me to sell because, if my clients pick up on my enthusiasm, they're
sold. Consumers are, in most cases, not really sure of their taste and if what they
like is good. My clients, loyal to me over a period, automatically become an extension of what I feel about art.

Tell us about the day-to-day running of an art gallery.

During a typical good day during the season, January, February, and March, I come in and put the coffee on, take a look at my show, and then, shortly thereafter, a client comes in and it becomes a social hour. We sit down and have a cup of coffee and she wants to see what we're showing. We get into dialogue and get excited to the point where she says she has to own it. Or maybe not, or maybe something else. And that happens throughout the day.

In addition to client contact, I talk with artists who want to show with me. They send me slides, they want to see me, and I never refuse to talk to them. Part of the fun is looking at all the art and deciding who you want to show. The artist might be wonderful, with beautiful art, but then you also have to evaluate whether or not you'll be able to sell it. Each space on the wall costs you *x* amount of money. You have to make your expenses and every inch of wall space must try to pay for itself.

You might also talk to the artist you're currently showing. Maybe for some reason his work isn't selling and then you have to console him.

You also have to concern yourself with the installation of a particular show and where a painting belongs in relation to another painting. Hanging the art is something you need to have a feel for. For instance, I have ten thousand square feet, five thousand feet on each level, so we have a big, expansive space to hang many different kinds of art. And it's very important to be able to hang an artist next to someone he's compatible with. You don't want any conflicts in image. You wouldn't want to put an ethereal kind of painting next to a very guttural abstract. You could destroy that very sensitive painting if it's within the view of something incompatible. You learn this on the job and through discussion and it's a gut feeling. There's no one book that can describe this. There is a sense that one feels.

While you have a show up, you're always anticipating and planning for the next show. I usually do a show for three weeks, then give myself a week off between shows. I don't usually do more than four shows a season. Then, after the shows, you bring out your own inventory, things you own outright that you have accumulated over the years.

It's been the most wonderful life for me. I can't tell you how great it's been. First of all I'm a painter, I play the violin, and I use my gallery for concerts. I come to work thinking I'm coming home. I'm going to where I want to be. I love the artists, I love selling important stuff, I love people responding to my enthusiasm. It's been glorious. I'm a very lucky guy—I love what I do.

What advice can you offer to those who are interested in working in or running an art gallery?

It's sometimes difficult to even get a job interview with the larger galleries. I never refuse to talk to anyone who is aspiring to get into the business—they can come in and pick my brain. Someone interested in pursuing a career in an art gallery should go talk to an established art gallery owner to get a feel for the business.

It's not an easy job; it's something that fails more than succeeds. Contacts are great to have before you start out. Even before you get your feet wet you should go to museums and speak to curators and directors. And, of course, go to the better galleries and make an appointment to have a dialogue, an informational interview, just to be really sure. If they're honest, they'll paint a true picture for you of what it's all about. If you want to chance it, then it's up to you, but at least you've given yourself that edge.

And if you want to open your own gallery—well, first you decide what you want to sell and promote. Being idealistic about it is one way to go, if you have faith in a particular artist but you know his work would be difficult to sell. Great art is not always palatable at first. Even Picasso, before he became famous, was laughed at by most of the people in the world. You have to be brave and have a conviction about the art, and that, of course, comes out of a love for it. You have to be sincere.

Rental of the space is the main factor. I would always look for a space in the best location, even though it might be more expensive. If you can be in a cultural area, near a museum, that is ideal. To look for a very inexpensive space off the beaten track is not the way to go.

Think of the cost of a year's rent. Other expenses are minimal. You have blank walls painted white, track lighting, a desk, and a little storeroom. There are advertising costs, brochures, announcements, your insurance, utilities, and any salaries you'll have to pay. That's the beginning.

Then you have to get a stable of artists who reflect your taste, who can help establish your image as a serious gallery.

In a craft gallery it might be easier to sell your inventory, but I wouldn't advise it as a way to get into serious art. If you get established as having a craft gallery, that's almost like a stigma. You always carry that on your back,

But it could be financially successful: people love crafts. Success on that level is easier than going for fine arts. More people will respond to a pot than a painting. You'll have a bigger audience.

The tragedy of the arts is that it caters to only 3 percent of the population. Now that could be quite a bit, if you're in a cultural area, but that 3 percent is distributed among the arts in general—music and arts—so if you want to hone in on just a segment of that, on just painting or just sculpture, there's not that much out there. You're in a minority arena. It's a risky business. But when something happens to have a magic combination—it's good and the public responds to it—that's paradise.

Matthew Carone is the owner of the Carone Gallery, a prestigious establishment in Fort Lauderdale, Florida. He handles mainly contemporary art, American, some European, and some Latin American paintings and sculpture. He is also an established painter himself and often is invited to show his work at other galleries. The Carone Gallery, a family business, has been in existence since 1957.

INTERVIEW

Elizabeth English
Art Curator

Elizabeth English, the artist and illustrator profiled in Chapter 2, also worked a stint as an art gallery curator.

How did you happen to become an art curator?

After doing the interior design for an innovative art gallery in downtown Boulder with a very wealthy, elite, and discriminating customer base, I was asked to curate their first art show for the opening of the gallery.

What skills are important for art curators to have?

Curating for an art gallery requires several abilities and considerations: a good eye for color and design; a knowledge of what potentially is going to sell to the public; a statement about how this gallery is different from other galleries and what its focus is; an awareness of local customer/client tastes and what other competing galleries are showing; an understanding of budgets and local sensibilities; a recognition of how the gallery is laid out, architecturally; proper lighting and view lines; correct and appropriate framing and matting of the artworks; and gallery spending limits.

If the gallery deals in prints and known artists, such as Old Masters or Impressionists, for example, one must also have a background in, and knowledge of, art history and of the artists' work displayed.

In a gallery that shows sculptures, one must also be aware of and have a good eye for spatial relationships. Another important asset is a knowledge of psychology and symbolism, as well as awareness of the emotional meanings of color, placement, juxtaposition, and design.

An important part of curating is being responsible for all aspects of the show, including selecting the artworks to be displayed; framing and matting the art; installing that art; working with the gallery owner(s) in designing the invitations to the opening and advertising in brochures, newspapers, and art magazines; and even choosing the food and wine to be served at the opening. Each and every element must be consistent, to provide a harmonious and corresponding ambiance to the exhibiting of the artworks for sale.

Each gallery is different, because of architectural layout, art focus of the gallery owners, customer base, and budget. A gallery of Southwestern art in Santa Fe will be curated differently from a gallery of antique prints and Old Masters in San Francisco, a gallery selling nautical arts and crafts in Boston, or a gallery showing only contemporary sculptures in Manhattan.

I chose to work on commission, as I was not a regular employee of the gallery and they had no money left after renovation to pay me to curate. I was also very confident that my curating would make the work sell, so I took 10 percent of the gross sales for the length of the show, and made out quite well on it. I'd also left a stack of my business cards at the gallery and got some more jobs doing interior design and curating when people saw my work.

What advice would you offer to potential curators?

Always keep in mind that the gallery exists to *sell* the art, not as a museum to merely showcase it! This means that you have to explain and depict to the viewers—by your placement, lighting, ambience, and mood of the show—why they should purchase the artwork and, once they buy it, display the art to its proper advantage.

INTERVIEW

Rodney Stephens
Framemaker

How did you get started in this business?

I started out picture framing part-time when I was going to architecture school. I was able to set flexible hours for myself. I have always enjoyed the presentation of artwork, the different mattings, styles, and techniques. My mother was an artist and she taught me about color and proportions. Plus I took several years of drafting in high school. It seems as if I have always known about basic matting, how the frame should complement the art work, correct proportions, the colors working together.

I started off at a frame shop in Albuquerque, New Mexico. I worked for a woman who had just taken over the shop and she was trying to run the shop and have a life at the same time. So she chose me to be manager of the business. She pretty much left me in charge of the shop and I had to learn as I went along.

I also read a lot of the how-to books on picture framing, which were very helpful. They give you the basics, how to miter a frame, for example, or how to cut a mat opening using a beveled knife. The shop was well stocked with tools so I learned how to cut the glass, to cut my own moldings, to cut the mattings, and to put the whole presentation together.

I worked for that business for approximately a year. When it changed hands and went in a different direction, I got a management position at a craft store in town that had a picture-framing division. I managed several people and was in charge of procurement and expediting of materials, quality control, customer service—the whole nine yards. That gave me the next level of training for the business side of things.

How would you describe framemaking?

There is a difference between a picture framer and a framemaker. A picture framer will most often work with stock frames—offering the basic picture framing services found in most communities, such as matting, dry mounting, and basic frame assembly. They work with some ready-mades and also offer a type of custom service.

But framemakers design and make their own hand-carved frames, with special moldings, rounded corners, gilding—work that is unique. It's considered the higher end of the profession.

I did a lot of conservation framing, preserving original artwork or delicate papers, much the way a museum does. I have framed everything imaginable: paintings, magazine covers, a baby dress, a baseball bat, medals, guns, a beer bottle collection, record albums, CDs, antique rugs, tapestries. The most unusual thing I framed was a composition of signed memorabilia from the Clinton presidential campaign for a local attorney who was involved with the campaign.

I had gallery space to present the type of framing work I did. I had an idea wall and a layout counter or composition table. Customers would bring a piece of artwork in. Maybe the customer would have some ideas already or they'd ask me for help. I had several thousand samples of mat board of every color, type, and texture. We'd first lay out the matting to establish a series—single, double, triple, and even more. Then after you get an idea of the matting you want to use you bring in the frame samples. I had frames from distributors and a line I made myself.

What are the positive and negative aspects of working as a framemaker?

The creativity was my favorite part of the job. I loved when a customer came in without a clue as to how to handle a particular item and looked completely to me for the design. The most enjoyable part was to take something simple and turn it into something magnificent—and then see the reaction of the customer when they came in to pick it up. That was the best part. Not everyone can envision that level of creativity.

The most difficult part of the work could be some of the customers—customers who would come into the store and ask for the cheapest thing we had. The word *cheap* to me refers to the type of work you do, not the price.

Another downside is that it's a seasonal business. Framing often falls into the category of home improvement, and most of that is done during the summer months. Frames make good gifts, too, so we'd do well during the holidays. But frames are not considered a necessity item. We'd have maybe six very strong months, but it can be difficult making a living doing this. You have to have a really good sense of humor for the slow times.

What advice can you offer to potential framemakers?

Those interested in pursuing this profession should get the trade magazines and learn about the trends in the industry. You can find them in libraries or on the Internet.

I also highly recommend going to a trade show in the industry. It's the best way to learn and see what is happening. You'll find manufacturers and distributors displaying everything from tools to picture frame samples.

Contacting the Professional Picture Framers Association (PPFA) is a good idea, too. They'll send you useful material on the profession. [Their address is listed in Appendix A.]

The qualities you'll need to succeed include creativity and being a self-starter. You also have to be willing to sacrifice a lot of personal time for business time. It's a very cutthroat competitive business, so you need to find your own niche, find something to make your business different.

Then make a good business plan. If you have to, hire a consultant to help you. Once you do that, find the best high-traffic location you can. That old saying, "Location, location, location," really matters.

Rodney Stephens started work as a framemaker part-time while he was attending architecture school. He opened his own shop in 1982 and closed it recently after more than fourteen years in the business. During his years in the industry he did framing work for private customers, art galleries, art alliances, museums, universities, and hospitals. He earned his B.A. in architecture from the University of New Mexico in Albuquerque in 1989.

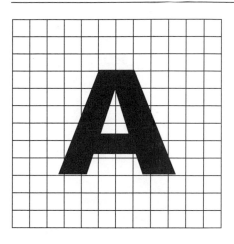

APPENDIX A: PROFESSIONAL ASSOCIATIONS

The following list of associations offers a valuable resource guide in locating additional information about specific art careers. Many of the organizations publish newsletters listing job and internship opportunities, and still others offer an employment service to members. A quick look at the organizations' names will give you an idea of their scope.

GRAPHIC ARTS

The American Institute of Graphic Arts
1059 Third Avenue
New York, NY 10021-7602

The Association of Medical Illustrators
1819 Peachtree Street NE, Suite 560
Atlanta, GA 30309-1848

Guild of Natural Science Illustrators
P.O. Box 652, Ben Franklin Station
Washington, DC 20044-0652

The National Association of Schools of Art and Design
11250 Roger Bacon Drive, Suite 21
Reston, VA 22090-5202

The Society of Illustrators
128 East 63rd Street
New York, NY 10021-7392

The Society of Publication Designers
60 East 42nd Street, Suite 721
New York, NY 10165-1416

FINE ARTS

American Arts Alliance
1319 F Street NW, Suite 500
Washington, DC 20004

American Craft Council
Information Center
72 Spring Street
New York, NY 10012

American Society of Interior Designers
608 Massachusetts Avenue NE
Washington, DC 20002-6006

Association for Living Historical Farms and Agricultural
    Museums
National Museum of American History
Room 5035
Smithsonian Institution
Washington, DC 20560

Costume Society of America
55 Edgewater Drive
P.O. Box 73
Earleville, MD 21919

National Assembly of Local Arts Agencies
927 15th Street NW, 12th Floor
Washington, DC 20005

National Assembly of State Arts Agencies
1010 Vermont Avenue NW, Suite 920
Washington, DC 20005

The National Association of Schools of Art and Design
11250 Roger Bacon Drive, Suite 21
Reston, VA 22090-5202

ART EDUCATION

American Association for Adult and Continuing Education
1101 Connecticut Avenue NW, Suite 700
Washington, DC 20036

American Association for Higher Education
One Dupont Circle NW, Suite 360
Washington, DC 20036

American Association of Christian Schools
P.O. Box 2189
Independence, MO 64055

American Association of Colleges for Teacher Education
One Dupont Circle NW, Suite 610
Washington, DC 20036

American Association of State Colleges and Universities
One Dupont Circle NW, Suite 700
Washington, DC 20036

American Federation of Teachers
555 New Jersey Avenue NW
Washington, DC 20001

Association for Childhood Education International
11141 Georgia Avenue, Suite 200
Wheaton, MD 20902

Council for American Private Education
One Massachusetts Avenue NW, Suite 700
Washington, DC 20001-1431

Council for Exceptional Children
1920 Association Drive
Reston, VA 22091

National Art Education Association
1916 Association Drive
Reston, VA 20191-1590

National Association for the Education of Young Children
1834 Connecticut Avenue NW
Washington, DC 20009-5786

National Association of Independent Schools
75 Federal Street
Boston, MA 02110

National Board for Professional Teaching Standards
300 River Place
Detroit, MI 48207

National Council for Accreditation of Teacher Education
2010 Massachusetts Avenue NW, 2nd Floor
Washington, DC 20036

National Education Association
1201 16th Street NW
Washington, DC 20036

MUSEUM STUDIES

African-American Museum Association
P.O. Box 548
Wilberforce, OH 45384

American Association for Museum Volunteers
6307 Hardy Drive
McLean, VA 22101

American Association of Museums
1225 Eye Street NW, Suite 200
Washington, DC 20005

American Institute for Conservation of Historic and Artistic
  Works
1717 K Street NW, Suite 301
Washington, DC 20006

Archives of American Art
Administrative Office
Smithsonian Institution
8th & G Streets NW
Washington, DC 20560

Association for Volunteer Administration
P.O. Box 4584
Boulder, CO 80306

Association of Art Museum Directors
41 East 65th Street
New York, NY 10021

Association of College and University Museums and Galleries
c/o University Museum
Southern Illinois University at Edwardsville
Edwardsville, IL 62026-1150

Association of Youth Museums
c/o Children's Museum of Memphis
1515 Central Avenue
Memphis, TN 38104

Canadian Museums Association
280 Metcalfe Street, Suite 400
Ottawa, ON K2P 1R7
Canada

Independent Curators Incorporated
799 Broadway, Suite 205
New York, NY 10003

Internship Program, Office of Museum Programs
Smithsonian Institution
Arts and Industries Building, Room 2235
Washington, DC 20560

International Association of Museum Facility Administrators
P.O. Box 1505
Washington, DC 20013-1505

International Institute for Conservation–Canadian Group
    (IIC–CG)
P.O. Box 9195
Ottawa, ON K1G 3T9
Canada

International Museum Theater Alliance
Museum of Science
Science Park
Boston, MA 02114-1099

Museum Computer Network
c/o Research and Scholar Office
National Museum of American Art
Smithsonian Institution
Washington, DC 20560

Museum Education Roundtable
P.O. Box 506
Beltsville, MD 20705

Museum Reference Center
Office of Museum Programs
Arts and Industries Building, Room 2235
Smithsonian Institution
Washington, DC 20560

REGIONAL MUSEUM ASSOCIATIONS

Mid-Atlantic Association of Museums
P.O. Box 817
Newark, DE 19715-0817

Midwest Museums Conference
P.O. Box 11940
St. Louis, MO 63112

Mountain-Plains Museum Association
Box 335
Manitou Springs, CO 80829

New England Museums Association
Boston National Historical Park
Charleston Navy Yard
Boston, MA 02129

Southeastern Museums Conference
P.O. Box 3494
Baton Rouge, LA 70821

Western Museums Conference
700 State Street, Room 130
Los Angeles, CA 90037

ART SALES

Art Dealers Association of America, Inc.
575 Madison Avenue
New York, NY 10022

Association of College and University Museums and Galleries
c/o University Museum
Southern Illinois University at Edwardsville
Edwardsville, IL 62026-1150

Professional Picture Framers Association (PPFA)
4305 Sarellen Road
Richmond, VA 23231

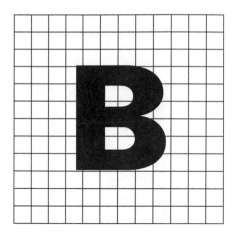

APPENDIX B: ART SCHOOLS

The following is a sampling of the hundreds of art schools or institutions with art departments that are in existence throughout the United States and Canada. Contact those with programs of interest to you for catalogs and more information. Where available, the school's website or E-mail address has been provided for you.

The Academy of Realist Art
5004 Sixth Avenue NW
Seattle, WA 98107
E-mail: realistart@aol.com
Traditional training in painting and drawing for contemporary artists. Classes are held in 10-week sessions, weeklong technical intensives, and weekend workshops. Figure drawing and painting, realist drawing, portrait, color theory, perspective, still life drawing and painting, and classes that introduce students to different media such as oil, watercolor, pastel, and color pencil.

Alberta College of Art and Design
1407 14th Avenue NW
Calgary, AB T2N 4R3
Canada
www.acad.ab.ca
B.F.A. in the visual arts and design including: ceramics, drawing, glass, jewelry, and metals, painting, printmaking, sculpture, textiles, interdisciplinary studies, photographic arts, and visual communications.

Alfred University
New York State College of Ceramics/School of Art and Design
Alfred, NY 14802
B.F.A. in art education and pre-art therapy, art history, ceramics,
     drawing, glass, graphic design, painting, photography,
     printmaking, sculpture, video arts, electronic imaging, and
     wood. M.F.A. in ceramics, glass, sculpture. B.A. in visual arts,
     performance, art history, and theory.

Arrowmont School of Arts and Crafts
556 Parkway
Gatlinburg, TN 37738
Arrowmont offers one- and two-week workshops in the spring
     and summer.

Art Academy of Cincinnati
1125 St. Gregory Street
Cincinnati, OH 45202
www.artacademy.edu
B.F.A. in fine arts (painting, drawing, sculpture, printmaking,
     photography) and communication design (graphic design,
     illustration, and photodesign); a B.F.A. with an emphasis in art
     history; an A.S. in graphic design; and an M.A. in art
     education.

Art and Learning Center
University of Maryland
0232 Stamp Student Union
College Park, MD 20740
http://www.inform.umd.edu/Student/Campus_Activities/Arts/Art
     _Center/
The University of Maryland Art and Learning Center offers
     noncredit courses for children and adults in pottery, painting,
     drawing, and photography. The classes run in the fall, spring,
     and summer semesters for up to 12 weeks.

Art Institute of Boston
700 Beacon Street
Boston, MA 02215
http://www.AIBoston.edu
B.F.A. in fine arts, photography, illustration, and design.

Art Institute of Southern California
2222 Laguna Canyon Road
Laguna Beach, CA 92651
www.aisc.edu
B.F.A. in drawing/painting, graphic design, and illustration.

Art Students League of New York
215 West 57th Street
New York, NY 10019
E-mail: h5294@netsgo.com

Associated Louisiana Artists
106 West Lawrence Street
Lake Charles, LA 70601
E-mail: ddentler@deltech.net
Visual arts classes in several media, held weekdays and evenings
    for adults in every level of experience. The Association also
    features a gallery for member exhibits and sales.

Associates in Art
5211 Kester Avenue
Sherman Oaks, CA 91411
http://www.associates-in-art.com/
Fine arts (drawing, painting, sculpture, printmaking), animation
    (traditional and computerized), illustration, and website
    design. The focus of the school is to prepare students with the
    skills to develop their own portfolios and compete for jobs in
    the Los Angeles area studio and advertising environment.

Atlanta College of Art
Woodruff Arts Center
1280 Peachtree Street NE
Atlanta, GA 30309
www.aca.edu
B.F.A. programs in communication design, drawing, electronic
    arts, interior design, painting, photography, printmaking, and
    sculpture.

Atlin Art Centre
P.O. Box 207
Atlin, BC V0W 1A0
Canada
E-mail: atlinart@netcom.ca
Offers three-week summer art courses to visual artists (painters,
    sculptors, photographers, and designers in the material arts)
    from intermediate to advanced.

Augusta State University
Fine Arts Department
2500 Walton Way
Augusta, GA 30904
E-mail: stu06160@aug.edu

B.A. and B.F.A. programs with concentrations in 3-D, 2-D, or general. Member of the University of Georgia system. Courses offered in drawing, painting, printmaking, high and low and primitive fired ceramics, casting, carving, installation, and survey and focus and contemporary art histories and art education.

Bard Graduate Center for Studies in the Decorative Arts
18 West 86th Street
New York, NY 10024
E-mail: jmaiorana@bgc.bard.edu
M.A. in history of decorative arts.

Boston University
School for the Arts / Visual Arts Division
855 Commonwealth Avenue
Room 552
Boston, MA 02215
B.F.A. in painting, sculpture, graphic design, and art education. M.F.A. in painting, sculpture, graphic design, art education, and studio teaching.

Brookfield Craft Center
Box 122
Route 25
Brookfield, CT 06804-0122
http://www.craftweb.com/org/brookfld/brookfld.shtml
National-profile nonacademic school for fine craftsmanship. Over four hundred classes and workshops with the nation's top artists/craftsmen.

California College of Arts and Crafts
5212 Broadway
Oakland, CA 94618
www.ccac-art.edu
Drawing/painting, printmaking, ceramics, glass, jewelry/metal, sculpture, textiles, wood/furniture, film/video/performance, photography, architecture, interior architecture, fashion design, graphic design, illustration, and industrial design.

California Institute of the Arts
24700 McBean Parkway
Valencia, CA 91355
Art, dance, film/video, music, and theatre.

Center for Creative Studies
201 East Kirby Street
Detroit, MI 48202-4034
www.ccscad.edu
B.F.A. degree in 17 majors in five departments: graphic
    communication, crafts, fine arts, photography, and industrial
    design.

The Center for Textile Arts
533 NE Davis Street
P.O. Box 1442
McMinnville, OR 97128
E-mail: cta@onlinemac.com
Offers a workshop-intensive environment in both contemporary
    and traditional forms of fiber mediums.

Centre des Metiers du Verre du Quebec
1200, rue Mill
Montreal, QC H3K 2B3
Canada
http://www.mtl.net/~cmvq/
Glass art studio offering academic courses, workshops, studio
    rental, exhibitions, general information on glass and glass
    artists from Quebec, Canada.

Claremont Graduate University
Center for the Arts
251 East 10th Street
Claremont, CA 91711-6182
http://www.cgu.edu/arts/art/mfahomepage.html
M.F.A. degrees. Personal instruction in private studios with leading
    contemporary artists. Degrees in all areas of studio practice.

Cleveland Institute of Art
University Circle
11141 East Boulevard
Cleveland, OH 44106
www.cia.edu
Ceramics, drawing, enameling, fiber, glass, graphic design,
    illustration, industrial design, interior design, medical
    illustration, metals, painting, photography, printmaking, and
    sculpture.

The College of New Jersey
Art Department
2000 Pennington Road
Ewing, NJ 08628-0718
http://www.TCNJ.EDU/~artmain/
The art department of the College of New Jersey offers the B.F.A.
    degree in graphic design and in fine arts and the B.A. degree
    in art education with numerous concentrations in the arts and
    design fields, such as computer graphics, art history, and
    photography.

Columbus College of Art and Design
107 North Ninth Street
Columbus, OH 43215-1758
www.ccad.edu
B.F.A. in advertising design, retail advertising, illustration,
    industrial design, interior design, photography, fine arts,
    package design, video, computer graphics, desktop publishing,
    fashion design, ceramics, glassblowing, printmaking,
    sculpture, and art therapy.

Contemporary Artists Center
Historic Beaver Mill
189 Beaver Street
North Adams, MA 01247
http://www.lifelong.com/CAC/
The Contemporary Artists Center is a not-for-profit summer artists'
    studio. Painting, sculpture, drawing, printmaking, photography,
    and mixed media. Studios are open 24 hours a day.

Cooper Union School of Art
30 Cooper Square
New York, NY 10003
http://www.cooper.edu/art.html
B.F.A. with concentrations in drawing, graphic design, painting,
    photography, printmaking, and sculpture.

Corcoran School of Art
500 Seventeenth Street NW
Washington, DC 20006-4899
http://www.corcoran.edu/
The Corcoran School of Art offers both degree and nondegree
    programs. The degree program is a full-time bachelor of fine
    arts curriculum with majors in fine arts, graphic design, and
    photography. The nondegree program offers more than 60
    classes of art-related courses to the general public.

The Deep Creek School
1417 S. Grandview Drive
Tempe, AZ 85281
http://www.asu.edu/cfa/art/events/deepcreek/DCS.html
Alternative summer art program in the Rocky Mountains near
    Telluride, Colorado. One five-week session each summer that
    explores issues in site-specific sculpture, digital media, and
    performance. University credit is available through Arizona
    State University.

Dodge Stained Glass Studio
737 Route 82
Hopewell Junction, NY 12533-6139
http://pages.prodigy.com/dodgestudio/
The classes focus on the copper foil technique.

Golden Gate University
Arts Administration
536 Mission Street
San Francisco, CA 94105
http://www.ggu.edu/schools/ls&pa/arts_admin/aa1.htm
The arts administration department at Golden Gate University was
    established as a graduate program in 1972 to train future
    managers and staff members of nonprofit visual and performing
    arts organizations, and arts service and funding institutions.

Haliburton School of Fine Arts
Sir Sandford Fleming College
Box 839
Haliburton, ON K0M 1S0
Canada
http://hal9000.flemingc.on.ca/fa/
The Haliburton School of Fine Arts runs for seven weeks each
    summer. Up to 40 art and craft courses, including painting,
    drawing, textiles, metal art, sculpture, and glass. Beginners to
    professionals are welcome. Visual arts courses specifically
    designed for teachers are also available.

Herron School of Art
Indiana University Purdue University Indianapolis
1701 North Pennsylvania Street
Indianapolis, IN 46202
http://www.herron.iupui.edu
B.A., B.F.A., B.A.E., and M.A.E. degrees in fine arts, visual
    communication, art education, and art history.

Indianapolis Art Center
820 E. 67th Street
Indianapolis, IN 46220
http://www.indplsartcenter.org/
Nonprofit, community-based art education facility offering over
    two hundred classes in each of three terms (fall, spring, and
    summer) annually. A variety of media including ceramics,
    watercolor painting, oil painting, metalsmithing, computer art,
    stone carving, photography, printmaking, drawing, and wood-
    working. Classes also available for children, aged 4 to 18.

Inspiration Farm
619 E. Laurel Road
Bellingham, WA 98226
http://www.nas.com/~gossamer/class.html
Summer glass workshops.

Johnson Atelier Technical Institute of Sculpture
60 Ward Avenue Extension
Mercerville, NJ 08619-3428
http://www.atelier.org
Johnson Atelier serves sculptors and artists worldwide, through
    educational programs, a fine art foundry, and supplies.

Kansas City Art Institute
4415 Warwick Boulevard
Kansas City, MO 64111-1874
www.kcai.edu
B.F.A. degree in illustration, design, fiber, ceramics, sculpture,
    photography and video, printmaking, and painting.

Kendal College of Art and Design
111 Division Avenue North
Grand Rapids, MI 49503-3193
B.F.A. in fine arts, furniture, illustration, industrial design,
    interior design, and visual communications.

Kent State University
School of Art
Kent, OH 44242
E-mail: glass9@mail.idt.net
Ceramics, glass, fiber, jewelry/metals, sculpture, painting,
    printmaking, graphic design, and art education. B.F.A. and
    M.F.A. degrees.

Loyola Marymount University
Department of Art and Art History
7101 West 80th Street
Los Angeles, CA 90045
http://www.lmu.edu/colleges/cfa/art/index.html
Art, design, and art history.

Maine College of Art
(formerly Portland School of Art)
97 Spring Street
Portland, ME 04101
www.meca.edu
Ceramics, graphic design, metals and jewelry, painting,
    photography, printmaking, sculpture, and art history.

Memphis College of Art
Overton Park
1930 Poplar Avenue
Memphis, TN 38104-2764
www.mca.edu
B.F.A. and M.F.A. degrees in design and fine arts.

Mendocino Art Center
45200 Little Lake Street
P.O. Box 756
Mendocino, CA 95460
http://www.mcn.org/a/mendoart/
The Mendocino Art Center is an educational, exhibition, and
    resource center for the visual and performing arts. Weeklong
    and weekend workshops in four major areas: fine arts,
    jewelry/metal arts, ceramics, and textiles.

Milwaukee Institute of Art and Design
273 East Erie Street
Milwaukee, WI 53202
www.miad.edu
B.F.A. in fine arts and design.

Minneapolis College of Art and Design
2501 Stevens Avenue South
Minneapolis, MN 55404
http://www.mcad.edu
Fine arts, media arts, design, and M.F.A. in visual studies.

Montserrat College of Art
23 Essex Street
Box 26
Beverly, MA 01915
www.montserrat.edu
B.F.A. and nondegree programs in painting, drawing,
    printmaking, photography, sculpture, graphic design,
    illustration, and art teacher certification.

Moore College of Art and Design
20th Street and the Parkway
Philadelphia, PA 19103-1179
www.moore.edu
Fashion design, communication arts—graphic design, illustration,
    and fashion illustration—fine arts 2-D, fine arts 3-D, interior
    design and textile design, and teacher certification.

More Fire Glass Studio
80 Rockwood Place
Rochester, NY 14610
http://www2.rpa.net/~morefire/
Evening classes, weekend workshops, and intensives in
    glassblowing, casting, flameworking, beadmaking, and
    sculpture.

The New England School of Art and Design
    at Suffolk University
81 Arlington Street
Boston, MA 02116
http://www.suffolk.edu/nesad/
A professional school of art and design with majors in interior
    design, graphic design, and fine arts.

New Orleans School of GlassWorks and Printmaking Studio
727 Magazine Street
New Orleans, LA 70130
http://www.primenet.com/~jmblair/home3.htm
A not-for-profit school specializing in handblown glass and
    printmaking.

New World School of the Arts
25 NE Second Street
Miami, FL 33132
The school offers a University of Florida B.F.A. in art and design.

New York Studio School
8 West Eighth Street
New York, NY 10011
Contact the school for a description of the school and courses.

The Ninety-Second Street Y School of the Arts
1395 Lexington Avenue
New York, NY 10128
http://www.92ndsty.org.
Offers community-based programs in dance, music, and the
    visual arts. A wide variety of artistic disciplines including:
    fine arts, ceramics, jewelry and metalsmithing, ballet, modern
    dance, and vocal and instrumental music. Two 13- and 15-
    week semesters, and a summer session.

North Seattle Community College
Art Department
9600 College Way North
Seattle, WA 98103
http://nsccux.sccd.ctc.edu/~humdiv/art/artdept.html
The art department offers professional training in the fine arts
    applicable toward college transfer or a terminal certificate of
    fine arts or an associate of fine arts degree. Continuing rotation
    of courses in painting, drawing, design, art history, ceramics,
    sculpture, watercolor, and jewelry design. All courses are
    geared to an 11-week quarter system in day and limited
    evening programs.

Northwest College of Art
16464 State Hwy 305
Poulsbo, WA 98370
http://www.nca.edu/
A 32-month B.F.A. degree program is offered in visual
    communication with majors in graphic design and fine arts.

Nova Scotia College of Art and Design
5163 Duke Street
Halifax, NS B3J 3J6
Canada
http://www.nstn.ca/nscad/
Contact the school for a description of the school and courses.

OCI School of Decorative Painting
3459 Finland Road
Pennsburg, PA 18073
E-mail: pdca148@ibm.net

Hands-on workshops in marblizing, woodgraining, and
wallglazing; two-day to two-week workshops.

Oregon College of Art and Craft
8245 SW Barnes Road
Portland, OR 97225
www.ocac.edu
B.F.A. and certificate programs in book arts, ceramics, drawing,
fibers, metal, photography, and wood.

Otis College of Art and Design
2401 Wilshire Boulevard
Los Angeles, CA 90057
www.otisart.edu
B.F.A. degree in 12 majors and an M.F.A. in painting, sculpture,
photography, printmaking, and video.

Pacific Northwest College of Art
1219 SW Park
Portland, OR 97205
www.pnca.edu
B.F.A. degree program, with majors in ceramics, graphic design,
general fine arts, illustration, individualized major, painting,
photography, printmaking, and sculpture.

Paier College of Art, Inc.
20 Gorham Avenue
Hamden, CT 06511
Contact the school for a description of the school and courses.

Parsons School of Design
66 Fifth Avenue
New York, NY 10011
www.parsons.edu
Fashion, product, interior, communication, illustration,
photography, architecture, fine arts, and design marketing.

Penland School of Crafts
P. O. Box 37
Penland, NC 28765
http://www.penland.org/
Books and paper, clay, drawing and painting, glass, iron, metals,
photography, printmaking, textiles, and wood.

Pennsylvania Academy of the Fine Arts
1301 Cherry Street

Room NE
Philadelphia, PA 19102
www.pafa.org
Drawing, painting, sculpture, and printmaking; B.F.A., M.F.A.,
certificate, and postbaccalaureate programs. Oldest art school
in the United States.

Pennsylvania School of Art and Design
204 North Prince Street
P.O. Box 59
Lancaster, PA 17608-0059
http://www.psad.org/
Three-year associate's degree programs in fine arts, graphic
design, and illustration.

Peters Valley Craft Education Center
19 Kuhn Road
Layton, NJ 07851
http://www.pvcrafts.org/
Blacksmithing, ceramics, desktop publishing, fiber, fine metals,
interior design, photography, weaving, and woodworking.

Pratt Fine Arts Center
1902 South Main Street
Seattle, WA 98144
Studios featured at Pratt include a hot-and-warm shop in glass, a
sculpture studio, a jewelry/metalsmithing studio, and a
printmaking/painting studio.

Pratt Institute
200 Willoughby Avenue
Brooklyn, NY 11205
http://www.pratt.edu
Architecture, art, and design.

Rhode Island School of Design
Two College Street
Providence, RI 02903
www.risd.edu

Ringling School of Art and Design
2700 North Tamiami Trail
Sarasota, FL 34234
http://vision.rsad.edu
B.F.A. in computer animation, fine arts, graphic design,
illustration, interior design, and photography.

Rochester Institute of Technology
College of Imaging Arts and Sciences
73 Lomb Memorial Drive
Rochester, NY 14623-5603
School of Art and Design: art education, graphic design,
    computer graphic design, interior design, industrial design,
    illustration, medical illustration, painting, and printmaking.
    School of American Crafts: ceramics and ceramic sculpture,
    metalcrafts and jewelry, woodworking and furniture design,
    weaving and textile design, glass.

Rocky Mountain Conservation Center
University of Denver
2420 South University
Denver, CO 80208
http://www.du.edu/rmcc/
The Rocky Mountain Conservation Center–University of Denver
    offers education programs in the field of art conservation.

San Francisco Art Institute
800 Chestnut Street
San Francisco, CA 94133
www.sfai.edu
B.F.A. and M.F.A. in film, painting, new genres, photography,
    printmaking, and sculpture/ceramics.

Santa Cruz Mountains Art Center
P. O. Box 911
Boulder Creek, CA 95006
http://www.enchantedcreek.com/slvculture/
Workshops in life drawing, watercolors, arts for children,
    ceramics, enameling, jewelry, moldmaking, and a broad range
    of media.

School of Art, Design, and Art History
San Diego State University
5500 Campanile Drive
San Diego, CA 92182-4805
http://psfa.sdsu.edu/school_of_art/index.html
B.A., M.A., and M.F.A. courses in fine arts, applied design,
    sculpture, design, and art history. The applied design programs
    include wood sculpture and furniture design, ceramics,
    metalworking and jewelry, and textiles.

School of the Art Institute of Chicago
37 South Wabash Avenue

Chicago, IL 60603
Art history and studio art.

School of the Museum of Fine Arts
230 The Fenway
Boston, MA 02115
http://www.smfa.edu
Contact the school for a description of the school and courses.

School of Visual Arts
SVA Galleries
209 East 23rd Street
New York, NY 10010
http://www.sva.edu
B.F.A. in advertising, animation, art education, art therapy,
    cartooning, computer art, film, fine arts, graphic design,
    illustration, interior design, photography, and video; M.F.A. in
    fine arts, illustration, computer art, and photography.

Sheridan College
School of Craft and Design
1430 Trafalgar Road
Oakville, ON L6H 2L1
Canada
http://www.sheridanc.on.ca/
Intensive training in four studio areas: ceramics, furniture,
    textiles, and glass. Additional studies in design, drawing,
    photography, craft history, and communications.

Skidmore College
Saratoga Springs, NY 12866
Painting, design, drawing, ceramics, graphics, jewelry,
    lothography, photography, watercolor, and fiber arts.

Spokane Art School
Center For The Visual Arts
920 North Howard
Spokane, WA 99201
Classes for adults and children in the visual arts including
    drawing, painting (in various media and levels), ceramics,
    jewelry, sculpture, and design.

Springfield Museum of Art Classes
107 Cliff Park Road
Springfield, OH 45501
E-mail: fwjames@spfld-museum-of-art.com

Classes include illustrating, basic drawing, calligraphy, oil and
watercolor painting, jewelry, stained glass, cartooning,
basketry, pottery, raku, life drawing and sculpting, art history,
and so on. Ages are from toddlers and preschoolers, to grade-
and high-school youth, to adults. Beginners and professionals.

Taos Art School
P.O. Box 2588
Taos, NM 87571
http://www.taosartschool.org/
The Taos Art School is a college-accredited institution offering
classes in painting, weaving, potterymaking, creativity, Native
American arts, basketry, and photography.

Thirdstone Art Works
3997 64th Street
P.O. Box 743
Saugatuck, MI 49453-0743
http://www.thirdstoned.com
Courses are offerred in flameworked glass (beadmaking and
small sculpture), stained-glass design and construction,
handmade paper, jewelry and metalworking, and drawing and
painting in many media.

University of Massachusetts—Dartmouth
College of Visual and Performing Arts
North Dartmouth, MA 02747-2300
Art history, art education, music, visual design, ceramics, jewelry
and metals, textile design and fiber arts, wood and furniture
design, painting, printmaking, and sculpture.

University of New Hampshire
Department of Art and Art History
Paul Creative Arts Center
30 College Road
Durham, NH 03824-3538
B.A. in studio art and art history; B.F.A. with emphasis in
painting, drawing, sculpture, photography, printmaking,
ceramics, furniture design/woodworking; minors in arts,
architectural studies; M.A. in teaching.

University of the Arts
Broad and Pine Streets
Philadelphia, PA 19102
Design, fine arts, media arts, crafts, dance, music, theater arts,
arts education, writing for media, and performance.

Vancouver Academy of Art
Office: 1404–1155 Harwood Street
Studios: 496 Prior Street
Vancouver, BC V6E 1S1
Canada
http://www.artacademy.com/
Intensive, part-time studies in drawing, painting, sculpture, and
     glass fusing.

Woodstock School of Art
Route 212
P.O. Box 338
Woodstock, NY 12498
http://www.bearsystems.com/wsa/wsa.html
Painting, drawing, sculpture, and printmaking.

Worcester Center for Crafts
25 Sagamore Road
Worcester, MA 01605
Ceramics, fiber, metals, and wood.

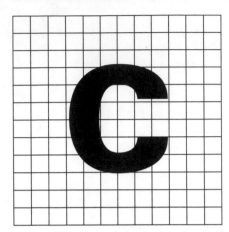

What follows is an alphabetical sampling of hundreds of museums and galleries in the United States and Canada. Individual addresses can be found by doing a search on the Internet, checking with your local library, or calling directory assistance in the particular city you're interested in.

These museums may be contacted for job, internship, or volunteer opportunities.

Abby Aldrich Rockefeller Folk Art Center—Williamsburg, Virginia

Academy of Art College Sculpture Center—San Francisco, California

Ansel Adams Center for Photography—San Francisco, California

Addison Gallery of American Art—Andover, Massachusetts

Adobe Krow Gallery—Bakersfield, California

African American Museum—Tacoma, Washington

Afro-American Historical and Cultural Museum—Philadelphia, Pennsylvania

Akron Art Museum—Akron, Ohio

Alaska State Museum—Juneau, Alaska

Albany Institute of History and Art—Albany, New York

Albrecht-Kemper Museum of Art—St. Joseph, Missouri

Albright-Knox Art Gallery—Buffalo, New York

Albuquerque Museum of Art, History and Science—Albuquerque, New Mexico

Aldrich Museum of Contemporary Art—Ridgefield, Connecticut

Alexandria Museum of Art—Alexandria, Louisiana

Allentown Art Museum—Allentown, Pennsylvania

Alternative Museum—New York, New York

Alyce de Roulet Williamson Gallery—Pasadena, California

Amarillo Museum of Art—Amarillo, Texas

American Craft Museum—New York, New York
American Museum of the Moving Image—Astoria, New York
Americas Society Art Gallery—New York, New York
Amerind Foundation Museum—Dragoon, Arizona
Amon Carter Museum of Western Art—Fort Worth, Texas
Anniston Museum of Natural History—Anniston, Alabama
Appleton Museum—Ocala, Florida
Architecture and Allied Arts Library—Eugene, Oregon
Arkansas Arts Center—Little Rock, Arkansas
Armand Hammer Museum of Art and Cultural Center—Los
    Angeles, California
Arno Maris Art Gallery—Westfield, Massachusetts
Arnot Art Museum—Elmira, New York
Art Center of Battle Creek—Battle Creek, Michigan
Art Complex Museum—Duxbury, Massachusetts
Art Council Gallery—Dutton Park, Queensland, Australia
Art Gallery of Greater Victoria—Victoria, British Columbia,
    Canada
Art Institute of Chicago—Chicago, Illinois
Art Museum at Florida International University—Miami, Florida
Art Museum of Santa Cruz County—Santa Cruz, California
Art Museum of South Texas—Corpus Christi, Texas
Art Museum of Southeast Texas—Beaumont, Texas
Art Museum of Western Virginia—Roanoke, Virginia
Arthur M. Sackler Gallery—Washington, DC
Artist's Museum—New York, New York
Arts Iowa City—Iowa City, Iowa
Arvada Center for the Arts and Humanities—Arvada, Colorado
Asheville Art Museum—Asheville, North Carolina
Asia Society Galleries—New York, New York
Asian Art Museum of San Francisco—San Francisco, California
Aspen Art Museum—Aspen, Colorado
ASU Art Museum—Tempe, Arizona
Athenaeum—Alexandria, Virginia
Attleboro Museum—Attleboro, Massachusetts
Bakersfield Museum of Art—Bakersfield, California
Baldwin-Wallace College—Berea, Ohio
Ball State University—Muncie, Indiana
Baltimore Museum of Art—Baltimore, Maryland
Balzekas Museum of Lithuanian Culture—Chicago, Illinois
Bank of America Galleries—San Francisco, California
Barnard's Mill Art Museum—Glen Rose, Texas
Baruch College/City University of New York—New York, New
    York
Bass Museum of Art—Miami, Florida
Bedford Gallery—Walnut Creek, California

Bellevue Art Museum—Bellevue, Washington
Bennington Museum—Bennington, Vermont
Bergen Museum of Art and Science—Paramus, New Jersey
Berkshire Museum—Pittsfield, Massachusetts
Betty Rymer Gallery—Chicago, Illinois
Bicentennial Art Center and Museum—Paris, Illinois
Birmingham Museum of Art—Birmingham, Alabama
Blaffer Gallery—Houston, Texas
Blanden Memorial Art Museum—Fort Dodge, Iowa
Boca Raton Museum of Art—Boca Raton, Florida
Boise Art Museum—Boise, Idaho
Bowdoin College Museum of Art—Brunswick, Maine
Bowers Museum—Santa Ana, California
Brandywine River Museum—Chadds Ford, Pennsylvania
Brattleboro Museum & Art Center—Brattleboro, Vermont
Brenau College Gallery—Gainesville, Georgia
Brevard Art Center and Museum—Melbourne, Florida
Brigham City Museum—Brigham City, Utah
Bronx Museum of the Arts—Bronx, New York
Brooklyn Museum—Brooklyn, New York
Bruce Museum—Greenwich, Connecticut
Buffalo Bill Historical Center—Cody, Wyoming
Butler Institute of American Art—Youngstown, Ohio
Cahoon Museum of American Art—Cotuit, Massachusetts
California Center for the Arts Museum—Escondido, California
California Museum of Art—Santa Rosa, California
California Museum of Photography—Riverside, California
Cambridge Multicultural Arts Center—Cambridge,
    Massachusetts
Cape Ann Historical Museum—Gloucester, Massachusetts
Cape Museum of Fine Arts—Dennis, Massachusetts
Carnegie Institute Museum of Art—Pittsburgh, Pennsylvania
Carson County Square House Museum—Panhandle, Texas
Cedar Rapids Museum of Art—Cedar Rapids, Iowa
Center for Creative Photography—Tucson, Arizona
Center for the Arts and Religion—Washington, DC
Center for the Fine Arts—Miami, Florida
Center for the Visual Arts—Oakland, California
Center of Contemporary Art (COCA) in North Miami—North
    Miami, Florida
County of Los Angeles Century Gallery—Sylmar, California
Chaffee Center for the Visual Arts—Rutland, Vermont
Chaim Goldberg Museum—Boca Raton, Florida
Charles A. Wustum Museum of Fine Arts—Racine, Wisconsin
Charles Allis Art Museum—Milwaukee, Wisconsin
Charles and Emma Frye Art Museum—Seattle, Washington

Charles B. Goddard Center for Visual and Performing Arts—
Ardmore, Oklahoma
Charles H. MacNider Museum—Mason City, Iowa
Charles Hosmer Morse Museum of American Art—Winter Park,
Florida
Chase Home Museum of Utah Folk Art—Salt Lake City, Utah
Cheekwood Museum of Art—Nashville, Tennessee
Cheney Cowles Museum—Spokane, Washington
Chinati Foundation—Marfa, Texas
Chrysler Museum—Norfolk, Virginia
Cincinnati Art Museum—Cincinnati, Ohio
City and County of Honolulu—Honolulu, Hawaii
Civic Fine Arts Center—Sioux Falls, South Dakota
Cleveland Museum of Art—Cleveland, Ohio
Cleveland State University Art Gallery—Cleveland, Ohio
Colorado Gallery of the Arts—Littleton, Colorado
Columbia Museum of Art—Columbia, South Carolina
Columbus Museum—Columbus, Georgia
Columbus Museum of Art—Columbus, Ohio
Contemporary Art Gallery—Vancouver, British Columbia, Canada
Contemporary Arts Center—Cincinnati, Ohio
Contemporary Arts Museum—Houston, Texas
Contemporary Museum—Honolulu, Hawaii
Cooper-Hewitt Museum—New York, New York
Coos Art Museum—Coos Bay, Oregon
Corcoran Museum of Art—Washington, DC
Corning Museum of Glass—Corning, New York
Craft and Folk Art Museum—Los Angeles, California
Cranbrook Academy of Art Museum—Bloomfield Hills,
Michigan
Crocker Art Museum—Sacramento, California
Cummer Gallery of Art—Jacksonville, Florida
Currier Gallery of Art—Manchester, New Hampshire
Dahesh Museum—New York, New York
Dahl Fine Arts Center—Rapid City, South Dakota
Dallas Museum of Art—Dallas, Texas
Danforth Museum of Art—Framingham, Massachusetts
Davenport Museum of Art—Davenport, Iowa
De Saisset Museum—Santa Clara, California
DeCordova Museum and Sculpture Park—Lincoln,
Massachusetts
DeLand Museum of Art—DeLand, Florida
Delaware Art Museum—Wilmington, Delaware
Denver Art Museum—Denver, Colorado
Des Moines Art Center—Des Moines, Iowa
Detroit Institute of Arts—Detroit, Michigan

Dixon Gallery and Gardens—Memphis, Tennessee
Doris Wainwright Kennedy Art Center—Birmingham, Alabama
Downey Museum of Art—Downey, California
Eastern Shore Art Center—Fairhope, Alabama
Edsel and Eleanor Ford House—Grosse Pointe Shores, Michigan
Eiteljorg Museum of American Indians and Western Art—
    Indianapolis, Indiana
El Museo del Barrio—New York, New York
El Paso Museum of Art—El Paso, Texas
Elisabet Ney Museum—Austin, Texas
Ellen Noel Art Museum—Odessa, Texas
Erie Art Museum—Erie, Pennsylvania
Evans-Tibbs Collection—Washington, DC
The Everhart Museum—Scranton, Pennsylvania
Everson Museum of Art—Syracuse, New York
Fayette Art Museum—Fayette, Alabama
Fayetteville Museum of Art—Fayetteville, North Carolina
Fine Arts Museum of Long Island—Hempstead, New York
Fine Arts Museum of the South—Mobile, Alabama
Fisher Collection—Pittsburgh, Pennsylvania
Fitchburg Art Museum—Fitchburg, Massachusetts
Fleischer Museum of American and Russian Impressionism—
    Scottsdale, Arizona
Florence Griswold Museum—Old Lyme, Connecticut
Florida Gulf Coast Art Center—Belleair, Florida
Florida International University Art Museum—Miami, Florida
Florida Museum of Hispanic and Latin American Art—Miami,
    Florida
Fort Wayne Museum of Art—Fort Wayne, Indiana
Frank Lloyd Wright Museum—Richland Center, Wisconsin
Franklin D. Murphy Sculpture Garden—Los Angeles, California
Fraunces Tavern Museum—New York, New York
Fred Sandback Museum—Winchendon, Massachusetts
Frederic Remington Art Museum—Ogdensburg, New York
Freeport Art Museum and Cultural Center—Freeport, Illinois
Freer Gallery of Art—Washington, DC
Fresno Art Museum—Fresno, California
Fresno Metropolitan Museum—Fresno, California
Frick Art Museum—Pittsburgh, Pennsylvania
Frick Collection—New York, New York
Fuller Museum of Art—Brockton, Massachusetts
Gadsden Museum of Fine Arts—Gadsden, Alabama
Gaston County Museum—Dallas, North Carolina
Genesee Country Museum—Mumford, New York
George E. Ohr Arts and Cultural Center—Biloxi, Mississippi
George Walter Vincent Smith Art Museum—Springfield,
    Massachusetts

Gertrude Herbert Institute of Art—Augusta, Georgia
Gibbes Museum of Art—Charleston, South Carolina
Glenbow Museum—Calgary, Alberta, Canada
Grand Forks Art Gallery—Grand Forks, British Columbia, Canada
Grand Rapids Art Museum—Grand Rapids, Michigan
Grants Pass Museum of Art—Grants Pass, Oregon
Greater Lafayette Museum of Art—Lafayette, Indiana
Greenville County Museum of Art—Greenville, South Carolina
Greenville Museum of Art—Greenville, North Carolina
Guggenheim Museum SoHo—New York, New York
Guild Hall Museum—East Hampton, New York
Heard Museum—Phoenix, Arizona
Hearst Art Gallery—Moraga, California
Heckscher Museum—Huntington, New York
Hibel Museum of Art—Palm Beach, Florida
Hickory Museum of Art—Hickory, North Carolina
High Museum of Art—Atlanta, Georgia
Hirshhorn Museum and Sculpture Garden—Washington, DC
Historic New Orleans Collection—New Orleans, Louisiana
History Museum of the Missouri Historical Society—St. Louis, Missouri
Honolulu Academy of Arts—Honolulu, Hawaii
Honolulu Advertiser Gallery—Honolulu, Hawaii
Hopi Cultural Center Museum—Second Mesa, Arizona
Hopper House—Nyack, New York
Hudson River Museum of Westchester—Yonkers, New York
Hunter Museum of Art—Chattanooga, Tennessee
Hunterdon Art Center—Clinton, New Jersey
Huntington Library, Art Collections and Botanical Gardens—San Marino, California
Huntsville Museum of Art—Huntsville, Alabama
Hyde Collection—Glens Falls, New York
Illinois Art Gallery—Chicago, Illinois
Illinois State Museum—Lockport, Illinois
Illinois State Museum—Springfield, Illinois
Indianapolis Center for Contemporary Art—Indianapolis, Indiana
Indianapolis Museum of Art—Indianapolis, Indiana
Institute of American Indian Arts Museum—Santa Fe, New Mexico
Institute of Contemporary Art—Boston, Massachusetts
International Center of Photography Midtown—New York, New York
International Center of Photography—New York, New York
International Institute for Modern Structural Art—Kansas City, Missouri
Isabella Stewart Gardner Museum—Boston, Massachusetts

Isamu Noguchi Garden Museum—Long Island City, New York
Islip Art Museum—East Islip, New York
J. Paul Getty Museum—Los Angeles, California
Jacksonville Art Museum—Jacksonville, Florida
James A. Michener Art Museum—Doylestown, Pennsylvania
Jane Voorhees Zimmerli Art Museum—New Brunswick, New
    Jersey
Janet Turner Print Gallery and Collection—Chico, California
Japan Society Gallery—New York, New York
J. B. Speed Art Museum—Louisville, Kentucky
Jersey City Museum—Jersey City, New Jersey
Jesse Besser Museum—Alpena, Michigan
Jewish Museum—New York, New York
Jim Savage Western Art and Gift Gallery and Memorial Studio—
    Sioux Falls, South Dakota
John and Mable Ringling Museum of Art—Sarasota, Florida
John F. Kennedy University Arts and Consciousness Galleries—
    Orinda, California
Joslyn Art Museum—Omaha, Nebraska
Judah L. Magnes Museum—Berkeley, California
Katonah Museum of Art—Katonah, New York
Kauai Museum—Lihue, Kauai, Hawaii
Kennedy Art Center Gallery—Oakland, California
Kentucky History Museum—Frankfort, Kentucky
Kimbell Art Museum—Fort Worth, Texas
Kirkpatrick Center Museum Complex—Oklahoma City,
    Oklahoma
Kitchener-Waterloo Art Gallery—Kitchener, Ontario, Canada
Klein Museum Art Gallery—Mobridge, South Dakota
Knoxville Museum of Art—Knoxville, Tennessee
Korean American Museum of Art and Cultural Center
    (KOMA)—Los Angeles, California
Laguna Art Museum—Laguna Beach, California
Laguna Gloria Art Museum—Austin, Texas
Lakeview Museum of Arts and Sciences—Peoria, Illinois
Laumeier Sculpture Park and Museum—St. Louis, Missouri
Lauren Rogers Museum of Art—Laurel, Mississippi
Leigh Yawkey Woodson Art Museum—Wausau, Wisconsin
LeMoyne Art Foundation: Center for the Visual Arts—
    Tallahassee, Florida
Light Factory Photographic Arts Center—Charlotte, North
    Carolina
List Visual Arts Center at MIT—Cambridge, Massachusetts
Long Beach Museum of Art—Long Beach, California
Longview Art Museum—Longview, Texas
Los Angeles County Museum of Art—Los Angeles, California

Louisiana Arts and Science Center—Baton Rouge, Louisiana
Louisiana State Museum—New Orleans, Louisiana
Louisville Visual Art Association—Louisville, Kentucky
Loveland Museum and Gallery—Loveland, Colorado
Lowe Art Museum—Coral Gables, Florida
Lyman Allyn Art Museum—New London, Connecticut
Madison Art Center—Madison, Wisconsin
Mariners' Museum—Newport News, Virginia
Maryhill Museum of Art—Goldendale, Washington
Masur Museum of Art—Monroe, Louisiana
Mattatuck Museum—Waterbury, Connecticut
Maude I. Kerns Art Center—Eugene, Oregon
Maurine and Robert Rothschild Gallery—Cambridge,
    Massachusetts
McAllen International Museum—McAllen, Texas
McNay Art Museum—San Antonio, Texas
Memphis Brooks Museum of Art—Memphis, Tennessee
Menil Collection—Houston, Texas
Meridian Museum of Art—Meridian, Mississippi
Metropolitan Museum of Art—New York, New York
Mexican Museum—San Francisco, California
M. H. de Young Memorial Museum—San Francisco, California
Miami University Art Museum—Oxford, Ohio
Michael C. Carlos Museum—Atlanta, Georgia
Mid-America Museum—Hot Springs, Arkansas
Midwest Museum of American Art—Elkhart, Indiana
Millicent Rogers Museum—Taos, New Mexico
Milton Art Museum—Milton, Massachusetts
Milwaukee Art Museum—Milwaukee, Wisconsin
Minnesota Museum of American Art—St. Paul, Minnesota
Mint Museum of Art—Charlotte, North Carolina
Mississippi Museum of Art—Jackson, Mississippi
Missoula Museum of the Arts—Missoula, Montana
Mitchell Museum—Mount Vernon, Illinois
Modern Art Museum of Fort Worth—Fort Worth, Texas
Montclair Art Museum—Montclair, New Jersey
Monterey Peninsula Museum of Art—Monterey, California
Montgomery Museum of Fine Arts—Montgomery, Alabama
Moody Gallery of Art—Tuscaloosa, Alabama
Morris Museum—Morristown, New Jersey
Morton B. Weiss Museum of Judaica—Chicago, Illinois
Moses-Kent House Museum—Exeter, New Hampshire
Muscarelle Museum of Art—Williamsburg, Virginia
Muscatine Art Center—Muscatine, Iowa
Museo de Arte Contemporanco—San Juan, Puerto Rico
Museo de Arte de Ponce—Ponce, Puerto Rico

Museo Italo-Americano—San Francisco, California

Museum of American Folk Art—New York, New York

Museum of American Glass at Wheaton Village—Millville, New Jersey

Museum of Art and Archaeology—Columbia, Missouri

Museum of Art, Fort Lauderdale—Fort Lauderdale, Florida

Museum of Arts and Sciences—Macon, Georgia

Museum of Arts and Sciences, Cuban Museum—Daytona Beach, Florida

Museum of Cartoon Art—Rye Brook, New York

Museum of Contemporary Art, Chicago—Chicago, Illinois

Museum of Contemporary Art—Los Angeles, California

Museum of Contemporary Art—North Miami, Florida

Museum of Contemporary Art, San Diego—La Jolla, California

Museum of Contemporary Art, San Diego—San Diego, California

Museum of Contemporary Religious Art (MOCRA)—St. Louis, Missouri

Museum of Early Southern Decorative Arts—Winston-Salem, North Carolina

Museum of East Texas—Lufkin, Texas

Museum of Fine Arts, Boston—Boston, Massachusetts

Museum of Fine Arts, Houston—Houston, Texas

Museum of Fine Arts—Santa Fe, New Mexico

Museum of Fine Arts, Springfield—Springfield, Massachusetts

Museum of Fine Arts—St. Petersburg, Florida

Museum of Fine Arts—Tallahassee, Florida

Museum of History and Art—Ontario, California

Museum of Holography/Chicago—Chicago, Illinois

Museum of Modern Art—New York, New York

Museum of Neon Art—Los Angeles, California

Museum of Northern Arizona—Flagstaff, Arizona

Museum of Northwest Art—La Conner, Washington

Museum of Oriental Cultures—Corpus Christi, Texas

Museum of Outdoor Arts—Englewood, Colorado

Museum of Photographic Arts—San Diego, California

Museum of the Americas, O.A.S—Washington, DC

Museum of the City of Mobile—Mobile, Alabama

Museum of the Hudson Highlands—Cornwall-on-Hudson, New York

Museum of the Plains Indian and Crafts Center—Browning, Montana

Museum of the Southwest—Midland, Texas

Museum of Western Art—Denver, Colorado

Museums at Stony Brook—Stony Brook, New York

Museums of Abilene—Abilene, Texas

Muskegon Museum of Art—Muskegon, Michigan

Nashville Parthenon—Nashville, Tennessee

Nassau County Museum of Fine Art—Roslyn Harbor, New York

National Academy of Design—New York, New York

National Gallery of Art—Washington, DC

National Museum of African Art—Washington, DC

National Museum of American Art, Renwick Gallery—
    Washington, DC

National Museum of American Art—Washington, DC

National Museum of the American Indian—New York, New York

National Museum of Women in the Arts—Washington, DC

National Portrait Gallery—Washington, DC

National Wildlife Art Museum—Jackson Hole, Wyoming

Nelson-Atkins Museum of Art—Kansas City, Missouri

Nevada Institute for Contemporary Art—Las Vegas, Nevada

Nevada Museum of Art—Reno, Nevada

Neville Public Museum of Brown County—Green Bay,
    Wisconsin

New Britain Museum of American Art—New Britain,
    Connecticut

New England Center for Contemporary Art—Brooklyn,
    Connecticut

New Jersey State Museum—Trenton, New Jersey

New Museum of Contemporary Art—New York, New York

New Orleans Museum of Art—New Orleans, Louisiana

New York State Museum—Albany, New York

Newark Museum—Newark, New Jersey

Newport Art Museum—Newport, Rhode Island

Newport Harbor Art Museum—Newport Beach, California

Niagara University—Niagara Falls, New York

Nicholas Roerich Museum—New York, New York

Nicolaysen Art Museum—Casper, Wyoming

No Man's Land Museum—Goodwell, Oklahoma

Nordic Heritage Museum—Seattle, Washington

North Carolina Museum of Art—Raleigh, North Carolina

North Country Museum of Arts—Park Rapids, Minnesota

North Dakota Museum of Art—Grand Forks, North Dakota

Norton Gallery of Art—West Palm Beach, Florida

Norton Simon Museum of Art—Pasadena, California

Noyes Museum—Oceanville, New Jersey

Oak Ridge Art Center—Oak Ridge, Tennessee

Oakland Museum—Oakland, California

Oakland Museum Sculpture Court at City Center—Oakland,
    California

Octagon Center for the Arts—Ames, Iowa

Ogunquit Museum of American Art—Ogunquit, Maine

Ohlone College Art Gallery—Fremont, California

Oklahoma City Art Museum—Oklahoma City, Oklahoma
Olana State Historic Site—Hudson, New York
Orange County Center for Contemporary Art—Santa Ana, California
Oregon School of Arts and Crafts—Portland, Oregon
Orlando Museum of Art—Orlando, Florida
Ormond Memorial Art Museum and Gardens—Ormond Beach, Florida
Oshkosh Public Museum—Oshkosh, Wisconsin
Otis School of Art and Design—Los Angeles, California
Owensboro Museum of Fine Art—Owensboro, Kentucky
Pacific Asia Museum—Pasadena, California
Paine Art Center and Arboretum—Oshkosh, Wisconsin
Palm Springs Desert Museum—Palm Springs, California
Palo Alto Cultural Center—Palo Alto, California
Paris Gibson Square Museum of Art—Great Falls, Montana
Parrish Art Museum—Southampton, New York
Paterson Museum—Paterson, New Jersey
Peabody Essex Museum—Salem, Massachusetts
Peabody Place Museum and Gallery—Memphis, Tennessee
Pennsylvania Academy of the Fine Arts—Philadelphia, Pennsylvania
Pensacola Museum of Art—Pensacola, Florida
Peppers Art Gallery—Redlands, California
Philadelphia Museum of Art—Philadelphia, Pennsylvania
Philbrook Museum of Art—Tulsa, Oklahoma
Phoenix Art Museum—Phoenix, Arizona
Plains Indians and Pioneers Museum—Woodward, Oklahoma
Plotkin Judaica Museum of Greater Phoenix at Temple Beth Israel—Phoenix, Arizona
Polk Museum of Art—Lakeland, Florida
Portland Art Museum—Portland, Oregon
Portland Museum of Art—Portland, Maine
Portsmouth Museums—Portsmouth, Virginia
Print Club of Albany and Museum of Prints and Printmaking—Albany, New York
Provincetown Art Association and Museum—Provincetown, Massachusetts
Purdue University Galleries—West Lafayette, Indiana
Queens Museum of Art—Queens, New York
Rahr-West Art Museum—Manitowoc, Wisconsin
Reading Public Museum—Reading, Pennsylvania
Redding Museum of Art and History—Redding, California
Rehoboth Art League—Rehoboth Beach, Delaware
The Renaissance Society—Chicago, Illinois
Reynolda House, Museum of American Art—Winston-Salem, North Carolina

Rice Museum—Georgetown, South Carolina
Richard L. Nelson Gallery—Davis, California
Richmond Art Museum—Richmond, Indiana
Riverchase Galleria—Birmingham, Alabama
Riverside Art Museum—Riverside, California
Roberson Museum and Science Center—Binghamton, New York
Rochester Art Center—Rochester, Minnesota
Rockford Art Museum—Rockford, Illinois
Rockwell Museum—Corning, New York
Rodin Museum—Philadelphia, Pennsylvania
Roland Gibson Gallery—Potsdam, New York
Rosenbach Museum and Library—Philadelphia, Pennsylvania
Roswell Museum and Art Center—Roswell, New Mexico
Rotunda and Hall of Fame Galleries—Tucson, Arizona
R. W. Norton Art Gallery—Shreveport, Louisiana
Sacred Heart University Gallery of Contemporary Art—Fairfield,
    Connecticut
Saginaw Art Museum—Saginaw, Michigan
Saint Louis Art Museum—St. Louis, Missouri
Salvador Dali Museum—St. Petersburg, Florida
San Angelo Museum of Fine Arts—San Angelo, Texas
San Diego Museum of Art—San Diego, California
San Francisco Craft and Folk Art Museum—San Francisco,
    California
San Francisco Museum of Modern Art—San Francisco, California
San Jose Museum of Art—San Jose, California
Sangre de Cristo Arts and Conference Center—Pueblo, Colorado
Santa Barbara Museum of Art—Santa Barbara, California
Santa Maria Museum Art Center—Santa Maria, California
Santa Monica Heritage Museum—Santa Monica, California
Santa Monica Museum of Art—Santa Monica, California
Schenectady Museum and Planetarium—Schenectady, New York
Schweinfurth Art Center—Auburn, New York
Seattle Art Museum—Seattle, Washington
Sheldon Jackson Museum—Sitka, Alaska
Sheldon Swope Art Museum—Terre Haute, Indiana
Sid Richardson Collection of Western Art—Fort Worth, Texas
Sioux City Art Center—Sioux City, Iowa
Sioux Indian Museum and Crafts Center—Rapid City, South
    Dakota
Slater Memorial Museum and Converse Art Gallery—Norwich,
    Connecticut
Solomon R. Guggenheim Museum—New York, New York
South Bend Art Center—South Bend, Indiana
Southeast Arkansas Arts and Sciences Center—Pine Bluff,
    Arkansas
Southern Alleghenies Museum of Art—Loretto, Pennsylvania

Southern Ohio Museum and Cultural Center—Portsmouth, Ohio
Southern Plains Indian Museum—Anadarko, Oklahoma
The Spartanburg County Museum of Art—Spartanburg, South
    Carolina
Springfield Art Museum—Springfield, Missouri
Springfield Museum of Art—Springfield, Ohio
St. John's Museum of Art—Wilmington, North Carolina
St. Johnsbury Athenaeum—St. Johnsbury, Vermont
Stamford Museum and Nature Center—Stamford, Connecticut
Stark Museum of Art—Orange, Texas
State Museum of Pennsylvania—Harrisburg, Pennsylvania
Staten Island Ferry Collection—Staten Island, New York
Staten Island Institute of Arts and Sciences—Staten Island, New
    York
Sterling and Francine Clark Art Institute—Williamstown,
    Massachusetts
Steven Oliver Art Center—Oakland, California
Storm King Art Center—Mountainville, New York
Studio Museum in Harlem—New York, New York
Sunrise Art Museum/Fine Art Museum—Charleston, West
    Virginia
Susquehanna Art Museum—Harrisburg, Pennsylvania
Tacoma Art Museum—Tacoma, Washington
Taft Museum—Cincinnati, Ohio
Tampa Museum of Art—Tampa, Florida
Telfair Museum of Art—Savannah, Georgia
Temple Museum of Religious Art—Cleveland, Ohio
Terra Museum of American Art—Chicago, Illinois
Textile Museum—Washington, DC
Third Floor Gallery—Chico, California
Thomas Gilcrease Institute of American History and Art—Tulsa,
    Oklahoma
Timken Museum of Art—San Diego, California
Tohono Chul Park—Tucson, Arizona
Toledo Museum of Art—Toledo, Ohio
Topeka and Shawnee County Public Library Gallery of Fine
    Arts—Topeka, Kansas
Trenton City Museum—Trenton, New Jersey
Triton Museum of Art—Santa Clara, California
Tucson Museum of Art—Tucson, Arizona
Turner Museum—Denver, Colorado
Tyler Museum of Art—Tyler, Texas
Ukrainian Institute of Modern Art—Chicago, Illinois
Ukrainian Museum—New York, New York
Union Galleries—Tucson, Arizona
University Gallery—Alexandria, Louisiana

University Memorial Center Gallery—Boulder, Colorado
University of Alaska Museum—Fairbanks, Alaska
University of Arizona Museum of Art—Tucson, Arizona
Vancouver Art Gallery—Vancouver, British Columbia, Canada
Virginia Museum of Fine Arts—Richmond, Virginia
Visual Arts Gallery—Birmingham, Alabama
Vizcaya Museum and Gardens—Miami, Florida
Wadsworth Atheneum—Hartford, Connecticut
Walker Art Center—Minneapolis, Minnesota
Walters Art Gallery—Baltimore, Maryland
Waterloo Museum of Art—Waterloo, Iowa
West Bend Art Museum—West Bend, Wisconsin
West Virginia State Museum—Charleston, West Virginia
Westmoreland Museum of Art—Greensburg, Pennsylvania
Whatcom Museum of History and Art—Bellingham, Washington
Wheelwright Museum of the American Indian—Santa Fe, New
    Mexico
Whistler House Museum of Art—Lowell, Massachusetts
Whitney Museum of American Art—New York, New York
Whitney Museum of American Art at Champion—Stamford,
    Connecticut
Whitney Museum of American Art at Philip Morris—New York,
    New York
Wichita Art Museum—Wichita, Kansas
Wichita Center for the Arts—Wichita, Kansas
Wichita Falls Museum and Art Center—Wichita Falls, Texas
William A. Farnsworth Library and Art Museum—Rockland,
    Maine
Wing Luke Asian Museum—Seattle, Washington
Woodmere Art Museum—Philadelphia, Pennsylvania
Woodstock Artists Association—Woodstock, New York
Worcester Art Museum—Worcester, Massachusetts
World Heritage Museum—Urbana, Illinois
The Wyeth Center—Rockland, Maine
Wyoming State Museum Art Gallery—Cheyenne, Wyoming
Yeiser Art Center—Paducah, Kentucky
Yellowstone Art Center—Billings, Montana
York Institute Museum—Saco, Maine
Your Heritage House Fine Arts Museum for Youth—Detroit,
    Michigan
Zanesville Art Center—Zanesville, Ohio
Zigler Museum—Jennings, Louisiana

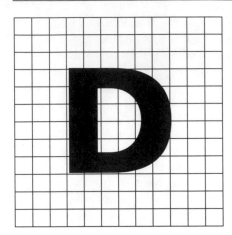

APPENDIX D: ART BOOKS

This appendix includes a sampling of books on the visual arts, listed alphabetically by title. The subjects may cover a particular medium, artist, or period. They are available through any bookseller.

About Looking. John Berger, J. Laslocky (editor). 1992.

Adam: The Male Figure in Art. Edward Lucie-Smith. 1998.

After the End of Art: Contemporary Art and the Pale of History. Arthur Coleman Danto. 1997.

After the Great Divide: Modernism, Mass Culture, Postmodernism (Theories of Representation and Difference). Andreas Huyssen. 1986.

Air Guitar: Essays on Art & Democracy. Dave Hickey. 1997.

American Century: Art and Culture, 1900–1950. Barbara Haskell. 1999.

Andy Goldsworthy: A Collaboration With Nature. Andrew Goldsworthy. 1990.

Annotated Guides: Annotated Art. Robert Cumming. 1995.

The Anti-Aesthetic: Essays on Postmodern Culture. Hal Foster (editor). 1999.

Art and Fear: Observations on the Perils (And Rewards) of Artmaking. David Bayles, Ted Orland (contributor). 1994.

Art and Illusion: A Study in the Psychology of Pictorial Representation. Ernst Hans Josef Gombrich. 1969.

Art and Objecthood: Essays and Reviews. Michael Fried. 1998.

The Art and Technique of Sumi-E: Japanese Ink-Painting As Taught by Ukai Uchiyama. Kay Morrissey Thompson. 1994.

Art and Visual Perception: A Psychology of the Creative Eye. Rudolf Arnheim. 1983.

Art As Experience. John Dewey. 1980.

Art in Theory 1900–1990: An Anthology of Changing Ideas. Charles Harrison (editor), Paul Wood (editor). 1993.

Art Is a Way of Knowing. Pat B. Allen. 1995.

Art, Mind, and Brain: A Cognitive Approach to Creativity. Howard E. Gardner. 1984.

Art Objects: Essays on Ecstasy and Effrontery. Jeanette Winterson. 1997.

The Art of Handpainting Photographs. Cheryl Machat Dorskind. 1998.

The Art of Painting Animals on Rocks. Lin Wellford. 1994.

Art on the Edge and Over: Searching for Art's Meaning in Contemporary Society, 1970s–1990s. Linda Weintraub. 1997.

The Art Pack—A Unique, Three-Dimensional Tour Through the Creation of Art over the Centuries: What Artists Do, How They Do It, and the Masterpieces. Christopher Frayling. 1993.

The Art Spirit: Notes, Articles, Fragments of Letters and Talks to Students, Bearing on the Concept and Technique of Picture Making, the Study of Art. Robert Henri, Margery A. Ryerson (editor). 1984.

The Arts and Human Development: A Psychological Study of the Artistic Process. Howard E. Gardner. 1994.

ArtSpeak: A Guide to Contemporary Ideas, Movements, and Buzzwords, 1945 to the Present. Robert Atkins. 1997.

Artists and Writers Colonies: Retreats, Residencies, and Respites for the Creative Mind. Gail Hellund Bowler. 1995.

The Artist's Guide to Selecting Colors. Michael Wilcox. 1997.

The Artist's Handbook of Materials and Techniques. Ralph Mayer, Steven Sheehan. 1991.

Artist's Manual: A Complete Guide to Painting and Drawing Materials and Techniques. Angela Gair (editor). 1996.

The Artists' Survival Manual: A Complete Guide to Marketing Your Work, Toby Judith Klayman, Cobbett Steinberg, 1996.

The Beginner's Guide to Acrylics: A Complete Step-by-Step Guide to Techniques and Materials. Angela Gair. 1997.

Believing Is Seeing: Creating the Culture of Art. Mary Anne Staniszewski. 1994.

The Best of the Joy of Painting with Bob Ross: America's Favorite Art Instructor. Annette Kowalski. 1995.

The Big Book of Decorative Painting: How to Paint If You Don't Know How—And How to Improve If You Do. Jackie Shaw. 1994.

Blimey!: From Bohemia to Britpop: The London Artworld from Francis Bacon to Damien Hirst. Matthew Collings. 1998.

Body Art: Performing the Subject. Amelia Jones. 1998.

A Book of Surrealist Games. Alastair Brotchie (editor). 1995.

Botero. Fernando Botero. 1997.

Chaim Soutine: An Expressionist in Paris. Norman L. Kleeblatt, Kenneth E. Silver. 1998.

The Complete Guide to Animation and Computer Graphics Schools. Ernest Pintoff. 1995.

Composition and Perspective: Lessons and Exercises to Develop Your Painting and Drawing Technique. James Horton. 1994.

Concerning the Spiritual in Art. Wassily Kandinsky, M. T. Sadler (designer). 1977.

Conversations in Paint. Charles Dunn. 1996.

The Creative Artist: A Fine Artist's Guide to Expanding Your Creativity and Achieving Your Artistic Potential. Nita Leland. 1993.

Creative Discoveries in Watermedia. Pat Dews. 1998.

Don't Just Applaud—Send Money!: The Most Successful Strategies for Funding and Marketing the Arts. Alvin H. Reiss. 1995.

Dynamic Light and Shade. Burne Hogarth. 1991.

Electronic Culture: Technology and Visual Representation. Timothy Druckrey (editor). 1997.

Farewell to an Idea: Episodes from a History of Modernism. T. J. Clark. 1999.

The Field of Cultural Production: Essays on Art and Literature. Pierre Bourdieu. 1994.

50 Secrets of Magic Craftsmanship. Salvador Dali. 1992.

The Geometry of Art and Life. Matila Costiescu Ghyka. 1978.

Goddess: A Celebration in Art and Literature. Jalaja Bonheim (editor). 1997.

Graphic Artists Guild Handbook: Pricing & Ethical Guidelines (9th ed). Graphic Artists Guild, Rachel Burd (editor). 1997.

Greatest Works of Art of Western Civilization. Thomas Hoving. 1997.

Helen Van Wyk's Favorite Color Recipes. Helen Van Wyk, Herbert Rogoff (editor). 1996.

Hirschfeld on Line. Al Hirschfeld. 1998.

History of Art. H. W. Janson. 1997.

How to Paint Like the Old Masters. Joseph Sheppard. 1983.

The Ice Palace That Melted Away: Restoring Civility and Other Lost Virtues to Everyday Life. William Stumpf. 1998.

Impressionism: Reflections and Perceptions. Meyer Schapiro. 1997.

Interactive Excellence: Defining and Developing New Standards for the Twenty-First Century. Edwin Schlossberg. 1998.

The Invisible Dragon: Four Essays on Beauty. Dave Hickey. 1994.

John Singer Sargent: Male Nudes. John Esten, Donna Hassler. 1999.

Landscape and Memory. Simon Schama. 1996.

Leonardo's Ink Bottle: The Artist's Way of Seeing. Roberta Weir. 1998.

Life, Paint and Passion: Reclaiming the Magic of Spontaneous Expression. Stewart Cubley, Michelle Cassou. 1996.

Living Color: A Writer Paints Her World. Natalie Goldberg. 1997.

Lure of the Local: Senses of Place in a Multicentered Society. Lucy R. Lippard. 1998.

Making Color Sing. Jeanne Dobie. 1989.

Mary Cassatt: Painter of Modern Women. Griselda Pollock, Mary Cassatt. 1998.

The Materials of the Artist and Their Use in Painting with Notes on Their Techniques of the Old Masters. Max Doerner, Eugen Neuhaus (translator). 1984.

Mexican Muralists: Orozco, Rivera, Siqueiros. Desmond Rochfort. 1998.

Michelangelo: The Vatican Frescoes. Pierluigi De Vecchi, Gianluigi Colalucci (contributor). 1997.

The Mission of Art. Alex Grey, Ken Wilber. 1998.

The Mustard Seed Garden Manual of Painting—Chieh Tzu Yuan Hua Chuan, 1679–1701: A Facsimile of the 1887–1888 Shanghai Edition with the Text Translated. Kai Wang, Mai-Mai Sze (editor). 1978.

The Mystery of Love: Saints in Art Through the Centuries. Sister Wendy Beckett. 1997.

No More Secondhand Art: Awakening the Artist Within. Peter London. 1989.

Nothing If Not Critical: Selected Essays on Art and Artists. Robert Hughes. 1992.

The 100 Best Small Art Towns in America: Discover Creative Communities, Fresh Air, and Affordable Living. John Villani. 1998.

100 Keys to Great Acrylic Painting. Judy Martin. 1995.

Oriental Painting Course: A Structured, Practical Guide to the Painting Skills and Techniques of China and the Far East. Jia Nan Wang. 1997.

Outside the Lines. Alexandra Nechita, Charles Osgood. 1996.

The Painted Word. Tom Wolfe. 1997.

Painting from the Source: Awakening the Artist's Soul in Everyone. Aviva Gold, Elena Oumano (contributor). 1998.

Painting What You (Want to) See. Charles Reid. 1987.

Paintings That Changed the World: From Lascaux to Picasso. Klaus Reichold, Bernhard Graf. 1998.

The Panorama: History of a Mass Medium. Stephan Oetermann. 1997.

Portraits: Talking with Artists at the Met, the Modern, the Louvre and Elsewhere. Michael Kimmelman. 1998.

The Power of Limits: Proportional Harmonies in Nature, Art, and Architecture. Gyorgy Doczi. 1994.

The Return of the Real: The Avant-Garde at the End of the Century. Hal Foster. 1996.

Techniques of the Observer: On Vision and Modernity in the Nineteenth Century. Jonathan Crary. 1992.

Three Thousand Years of Chinese Painting. Richard M. Barnhart (editor). 1997.

Tiffany's 20th Century: A Portrait of American Style. John Loring. 1997.

Titian's Women. Rona Goffen. 1997.

To Paint Her Life: Charlotte Salomon in the Nazi Era. Mary Lowenthal Felstiner. 1997.

Uncontrollable Beauty: Toward a New Aesthetics. Bill Beckley (editor), David Shapiro (editor). 1998.

The Unknown Matisse: A Life of Henri Matisse: The Early Years, 1869–1908. Hilary Spurling. 1998.

Van Gogh: The Complete Paintings. Ingo F. Walther, R. Metzger (contributor). 1994.

Van Gogh's Van Goghs: Masterpieces from the Van Gogh Museum, Amsterdam. Richard Kendall. 1998.

Velazquez: The Technique of Genius. Jonathan Brown. 1998.

Venetian Glass: Confections in Glass 1855–1914. Sheldon Barr. 1998.

Vision and Painting: The Logic of the Gaze. Norman Bryson. 1986.

Your Painting Questions Answered from A to Z. Helen Van Wyk. 1997.

Ways of Seeing. John Berger. 1995.

What Painting Is: How to Think about Oil Painting, Using the Language of Alchemy. James Elkins. 1998.

A Worldly Art: The Dutch Republic 1585–1718. Mariet Westermann. 1996.

The Zen of Creative Painting: An Elegant Design for Revealing Your Muse. Jeanne Carbonetti. 1998.

APPENDIX E: ART FAIRS AND EXPOS

The following list is a sampling of art fairs and expos where art lovers can view and purchase art and where artists can sell their work. Use the E-mail or contact addresses provided for information on dates, times, and specific locations.

Around the Coyote Art Festival
1579 N. Milwaukee
Second Floor
Chicago, IL 60622
E-mail: aroundthecoyote@hotmail.com
Dedicated to highlighting the work of resident artists in two
    Chicago neighborhoods and to reunifying the community by
    working with local organizations to form collaborative
    educational programs.

Broad Ripple Art Fair
820 E. 67th Street
Indianapolis, IN 46220
E-mail: inartctr@netdirect.net
http://www.indplsartcenter.org/
More than two hundred artists show and sell their fine art and fine
    craft work in a park-like setting. Other activities include
    music, a children's area, a gourmet food court, and the
    opportunity to explore the year-round activities of the
    Indianapolis Art Center.

Brookline Artists' Open Studios
Brookline, MA 02467
E-mail: starbrook@earthlink.net

http://www.brooklineart.cjb.net/
Annual open studios event for participating Brookline artists.
    Sponsored by the Brookline Council for Art and Humanities
    and Massachusetts Cultural Council.

Carefree Fine Art and Wine Festival
Thunderbird Artists
15648 N. Eagles Nest Drive
Fountain Hills, AZ 85268
E-mail: thunderbirdart@hotmail.com
Carefree is in the Sonoran Desert, 20 minutes north of Scottsdale.
    The streets of Carefree are closed and turned into a festival
    that includes 165 juried artists, wine and microbrew tastings,
    and musical entertainment.

Celebration of Fine Art
Scottsdale Road
Scottsdale, AZ 84254
E-mail: ArtTents@aol.com
http://www.arizonaguide.com/celebrateart/
Artists from across the country exhibit in a variety of media
    including: oil, watercolor, sculpture, photography, jewelry,
    ceramics, baskets, furniture, and contemporary mixed media.
    A sculpture exhibition with life-size and monumental
    sculpture is located in the central courtyard of the show. This
    is a unique event that combines the casual and relaxed
    atmosphere of a street fair with the high quality art found in an
    art gallery.

Central Pennsylvania Festival of the Arts
P.O. Box 1023
State College, PA 16804
E-mail: jwc@arts-festival.com
http://www.arts-festival.com/
The Central Pennsylvania Festival of the Arts is a nonprofit
    corporation, to celebrate the arts. The event is held the second
    weekend in July in downtown State College and on the campus
    of Penn State University, and features the work of
    approximately 350 artists from the United States and Canada.

Cleveland Christmas Connection
P.O. Box 45395
Cleveland, OH 44145
E-mail: christmasinc@juno.com
More than nine hundred booths of arts, crafts, retail, and
    decorating items for sale.

Cleveland Springtime Connection
P.O. Box 45395
Cleveland, OH 44145
E-mail: christmasinc@juno.com
Four hundred booths of arts, crafts, retail, and spring decorating
    items.

Festival of Arts
Pageant of the Masters
P.O. Box 37
Newport Beach, CA 92652
E-mail: todd@newportinternet.com
Annual exhibit of original artworks.

Freedom Festival
Blue Ridge Artists and Crafters Association
P.O. Box 1033
Waynesville, NC 28786
E-mail: doug@webtv.net
Held at Haywood County Fairgrounds, Route 209, Lake
    Junaluska, North Carolina.

Heart of Virginia Festival
P.O. Box 35
Farmville, VA 23901
E-mail: info@heartofvirginia.org
http://www.heartofvirginia.org/
A celebration of the arts, culture, and music of Southside Virginia
    held in Farmville, Virginia.

Mable House Artfest
Mable House
5239 Floyd Road
Mableton, GA 30126
http://www.artshow.com/MableHouse/artfestnew.html
An outdoor festival featuring fine arts, country crafts, art and
    craft demonstrations, children's activities, entertainment, and
    food concessions with a focus on the heritage of the
    community. Sponsored by the South Cobb Arts Alliance in
    conjunction with Cobb County Parks, Recreation, and Cultural
    Affairs.

The McKinney Avenue Contemporary Jurored Exhibition
3120 McKinney Avenue
Dallas, TX 75204
E-mail: mary@the-mac.org

http://www.themac.net/
This juried exhibition is open to Texas residents. Cash prizes.

Melbourne Art Festival
P.O. Box 611
Melbourne, FL 32902
E-mail: info@melbournearts.org
http://www.melbournearts.org/
Held every year during the fourth weekend in April. The two-day
    festival features 250 artists working in graphics, sculpture,
    painting, photography, jewelry, ceramics, and other media.

Pacific Northwest Arts Fair
Bellevue Art Museum
301 Bellevue Square
Bellevue, WA 98004
E-mail: bam@bellevueart.org
http://www.bellevueart.org/
Features more than three hundred U.S. and Canadian artists
    selected by an independent jury.

Photo L.A.
The 8th Los Angeles Print Exposition
Butterfield and Butterfield
7601 Sunset Boulevard
Los Angeles, CA 90046
E-mail: stephen@stephencohengallery.com
http://www.stephencohengallery.com/photola/frame4.html
The largest and longest running photographic art fair in the West.

Renaissance in Rehoboth
210 Savannah Road
Lewes, DE 19958
E-mail: art@rehobothtoday.com
http://www.rehobothtoday.com/Renaissance/
Renaissance in Rehoboth is a nine-week celebration of art taking
    place throughout the entire Delaware coastal region.

Seaside Fine Art Exposition
Seaside Civic and Convention Center
415 First Avenue
Seaside, OR 97138
E-mail: info@artshows.net
http://www.artshows.net/

More than 50 artists exhibiting original works of fine arts in two- and three-dimensional formats.

Skokie Art Guild's 38th Annual Art Fair
6704 N. Trumbull Avenue
Lincolnwood, IL 60645
E-mail: skokieart@aol.com
Fine art fair with more than 65 exhibitors.

Spirit of Art Festival
Delaware Foundation for the Visual Arts
2205 Elmfield Road
Wilmington, DE 19810-2719
E-mail: conawayg@magpage.com
An outdoor, juried, booth show on the grounds of the Delaware Museum of Natural History in Wilmington, Delaware.

Three Rivers Arts Festival
707 Penn Avenue
Pittsburgh, PA 15222
E-mail: kerri@sgi.net
http://www.artswire.org/traf/
An annual visual and performing arts festival located in downtown Pittsburgh. The 17-day-long festival includes a juried visual arts exhibition, an artists' market with more than four hundred crafters and artists, daily performances on five stages, and exhibitions of local and national artists in various indoor and outdoor sites throughout downtown Pittsburgh and Point State Park.

Watermedia
Pikes Peak Watercolor Society
214 N. Institute Street
Colorado Springs, CO 80903
E-mail: ppwart@pcisys.net
http://www.pcisys.net/~ppwsart/
International juried exhibit and show that is held at a different location in the Pikes Peak region of Colorado each year.

The Western Design Conference
Suite 105
1108 W. 14th Street
Cody, WY 82414
E-mail: info@westd.org
http://www.westd.org/

A gathering of lovers of Western design—furniture makers, decorators, fashion designers, scholars, and craftsmen. An invitation-only, juried exhibition is the centerpiece of the conference with more than 50 craftsmen and fashion designers submitting their finest work of both traditional and contemporary Western design. The conference also includes seminars for craftsmen. Held concurrently with the Buffalo Bill Art Show and Buffalo Bill Historical Center's Patron's Ball.